GREAT WAR LITERATURE

NOTES

Written by W Lawrance

on

THE FIRST CASUALTY

A NOVEL BY BEN ELTON

Great War Literature Notes on The First Casualty, a novel by Ben Elton.
Written by W Lawrance

Published by:
Great War Literature Publishing LLP
Forum House, Stirling Road, Chichester, PO19 7DN
Web site: *www.greatwarliterature.co.uk*
E-Mail: *admin@greatwarliterature.co.uk*

Produced in Great Britain

First Published as e-book 2011
This Edition published 2014. Copyright ©2005-2104 Wendy Lawrance.
The moral right of the author has been asserted.

ISBN 978-1910603116 Paperback Edition

10 9 8 7 6 5 4 3 2 1

Design and production by Great War Literature Publishing LLP
Typeset in Neue Helvetica, ITC Berkeley Old Style and Trajan Pro

Great War Literature Notes on

The First Casualty

CONTENTS

Preface	5
Introduction	7
Synopsis	9
Chapters 1-5	9
Chapters 6-10	14
Chapters 11-15	18
Chapters 16-20	22
Chapters 21-25	25
Chapters 26-30	27
Chapters 31-35	31
Chapters 36-40	34
Chapters 41-45	39
Chapters 46-50	44
Chapters 51-52	50
Character Analysis	55
Douglas Kingsley	55
Captain Shannon	59
Nurse Kitty Murray	62
Themes	65
Murder and Justice	65
The Question of Truth	69
Comparisons	73
The Portrayal of Conscientious Objectors	73
Language and Writing Style	78
Further Reading Recommendations	89
Bibliography	97
Other Titles	99

PREFACE

The primary purpose of Great War Literature Study Guides is to provide in-depth analysis of First World War literature for GCSE and A-Level students.

Great War Literature Publishing have taken the positive decision to produce a uniquely detailed and in-depth interpretation of selected works for students. We also actively promote the publication of our works in an electronic format via the Internet to give the broadest possible access.

Our publications can be used in isolation or in collaboration with other study guides. It is our aim to provide assistance with your understanding of First World War literature, not to provide the answers to specific questions. This approach provides the resources that allow the student the freedom to reach their own conclusions and express an independent viewpoint.

The structure of Great War Literature Study Guides allows the reader to delve into a required section easily without the need to read from beginning to end.

The Great War Literature Study Guides have been thoroughly researched and are the result of over 30 years of experience of studying this particular genre.

Studying literature is not about being right or wrong, it is entirely a matter of opinion. The secret to success is developing the ability to form these opinions and to deliver them succinctly and reinforce them with quotes and clear references from the text.

Great War Literature Study Guides help to extend your knowledge of First World War literature and offer clear definitions and guidance to enhance your studying. Our clear and simple layouts make the guides easy to access and understand.

The Great War Literature A-Level Study Guide on *The First Casualty*, provides a critical assessment of many aspects of this novel and is based entirely on the opinion of the author of this guide.

INTRODUCTION

This is an unusual study guide for an unusual First World War novel, for the very simple reason that, in my opinion, it is not primarily, a conventional First World War novel at all. It is really a murder mystery that just happens to be set in 1917, amidst the mud and blood of Flanders. However, for some reason that escapes my understanding, at least one major examining board has placed this novel on their study list and we have received several requests, from teachers and students, for a study guide to accompany the text.

This is evidently Ben Elton's first serious novel and it must clearly be acknowledged that when he wrote it, he had no idea that several years later, students would be reading it and analysing it as part of their A-Level syllabus. Having said that, Pat Barker, Sebastian Faulks and Susan Hill had no notion that their novels would be similarly studied either. However, in this case, I really do get the impression that the war is the setting, rather than the focus and that for this novel to be anywhere on the reading lists within this genre, is a mistake.

The study guide which I have, therefore, written is very different to any other which I have written before and there are reasons for this, which I would like the opportunity to explain. This novel has many shortcomings when compared with other, more traditional, First World War novels: the plot, characters, research, historical and factual accuracy are flimsy. Therefore in many sections within this study guide, although I have provided a conventional analysis, as I normally would, I have gone on to provide a more critical appraisal as well.

I do not feel,however, that Ben Elton ever intended that his novel should be analysed and picked apart in this fashion, so while I acknowledge that many of my criticisms are quite cutting, I have also tried to keep them humourous where possible, partly because the inclusion of this novel on the syllabus is something which I cannot take too seriously.

If Mr Elton, or anyone else for that matter, is offended by any of my comments, I apologise and point out that, as with all of my study guides, these words are only my opinion.

W Lawrance
November 2014

THE FIRST CASUALTY
BY BEN ELTON

SYNOPSIS

INTRODUCTION

As this is a novel of 52 Chapters, I have broken it down into sections of five chapters each. These sections are followed by a Critical Analysis of the content of each of these five chapters, in turn. This has been done in sections, rather than producing a single Critical Analysis section at the end of the Study Guide, as I normally do, for the obvious reason, that there is, in my opinion, quite a lot upon which to comment and the Critical Analysis Section would, therefore, hardly be termed as 'bitesize'!

CHAPTERS 1-5

Chapter 1

In the Ypres Salient in October 1917, a man, laden down with an enormous reel of barbed wire trudges along the duckboards, daring not to lose his footing, as the swampy ground either side of him will just swallow up any who stray from the pathways. Behind him, an officer from the Military Police tries to make his way through, but cannot be heard and so is forced to follow along behind this man. Suddenly, however, the man stumbles and falls from the duckboards, disappearing into the mud in a 'moment'.

Chapter 2

Douglas Kingsley, an Inspector in the Metropolitan Police, is being tried for conscientious objection. He appears in court in full uniform and cuts a fine figure, although he and the Judge are soon at loggerheads, as the latter objects to Kingsley's arrogant attitude towards both the court itself and the matter in hand. The public also cry out against Kingsley, calling him a coward and the policeman wonders whether his own brother, Robert, would have reacted similarly, had he not gone missing on The Somme.

Kingsley's objections to the war are not moral or religious, but intellectual - grounds which even he realises cannot be upheld. Despite the inevitable cost to himself and his family, however, Kingsley continues to argue his case, which the Judge finds ridiculous.

Chapter 3

While awaiting sentencing in prison, Kingsley receives a visit from his wife, Agnes. We learn about the background to their courtship and marriage: Agnes Beaumont had been the beautiful daughter of the Commissioner of Scotland Yard. Kingsley had decided that, despite their differences and against the advice of his friends, Agnes was the woman for him and he had pursued her. Now her visit to him in prison signifies a final goodbye, no less distressing to Kingsley than when Agnes had abandoned their 'marriage bed', leaving behind nothing but a white feather to show her opinion of her husband's actions.

Agnes tells Kingsley that she will be seeking a divorce; she berates him harshly for his decision and informs him of the consequences which have already taken place within their household and which will probably continue to affect the family well into the future. They argue bitterly over Kingsley's stance, which Agnes compares to that of the many other men who are fighting and dying to protect the country they love. Just before she leaves, Agnes tells Kingsley that she still loves him; she returns her wedding ring and obtains his permission to change their son's surname once their divorce has been finalised.

Chapter 4

In the Lavender Lamp Club in London, also known as Bartholomew's Private Hotel, a group of young homosexual men are meeting. Among them is Captain

Abercrombie (a Viscount in private life), a poet and decorated officer, who is about to return to France. Abercrombie meets another young officer, named Stamford, who is about to join the same regiment for the first time, and who is extremely nervous at the prospect. Stamford has written some poetry, but Abercrombie refuses to read it, claiming to have given up on poetry some time earlier. The two men drink and dance together, before going upstairs to the more private rooms.

Chapter 5

In the small Belgian village of Wytschaete, two miles behind the front lines, the men of the 5th Battalion, East Lancashire Regiment are lining up for a shower. They talk and joke as they wait for their turn and some of the older men explain to the newcomers how much times have changed, in that they used to be given back their own uniforms after a bath, whereas now they must take pot luck, which they all find demeaning. One of the men, named Hopkins, is especially outspoken and is renowned among the men for his communist sympathies, which make him unpopular. After their shower, which they all seem to enjoy, Hopkins is outraged at the condition of the uniform, which he is given to wear and refuses to put on the garments. Eventually, he is led away by the officer in charge, for refusing to obey an order.

Critical Appraisal of Chapters 1-5

The first chapter sets the scene for what is to follow very much later in the novel, but is also, essentially, a platform, by which the author may introduce one of his overriding motifs: the appalling plight of the 'poor bloody infantry', during the First World War. One has to question, however, whether the soldier would really have disappeared into the mud in a 'moment'. In her book, They Called It Passchendaele, Lyn MacDonald's contributing veterans make numerous references to the mud, rain, slime and swamps of the battlefields surrounding that now infamous village. There are a couple of descriptions of men becoming trapped in the mud, one for over four days and another, whose death is described as follows: 'He went down gradually. He kept begging us to shoot him... Who could shoot him? We stayed with him, watching him go down in the mud. And he died.' Personally, I find this account, given by Sergeant T. Berry DCM, of the 1st Battalion, The Rifle Brigade, much more poignant and engaging, than to be merely told that a man died in a 'moment'. Ben Elton could have described the man's appearance; the fear in his eyes as he attempted to free himself, his arms flailing helplessly; the reaction of those around him as they either fought to rescue him, or did nothing, knowing that a rescue would be futile. He could have described the expressions on the faces of the men who watched him drown in the mud, knowing that they might be next. He could have transported us to the very hell of Passchendaele in that first chapter: he could have given us so much more than just a 'moment'.

The subtitle of chapter two: 'some time earlier' is somewhat vague and rather suggests that the author could not be bothered to calculate an accurate chronology. During the 'trial' that forms this chapter, Kingsley argues his logical and intellectual reasons against participating in the conflict, although I personally doubt that a police officer of his rank would have been conscripted anyway. His arguments are quite similar to those put forward by Siegfried Sassoon in the Declaration which he made in 1917, especially insofar as they relate to Great Britain's treaty with Belgium and its relevance to the conflict. There are many flaws, omissions and conveniences with regard to Kingsley's arrest, imprisonment and trial (many of which will be studied in greater detail in later chapters of this guide). These have essentially been employed because it is necessary to the plot that Kingsley should be in prison.

Another 'convenience' arrives in Chapter three, in the shape of Agnes, who turns out to be the daughter of the Commissioner of Scotland Yard, which seems more than a little contrived, as does the introduction of the giving of white feathers to those accused of cowardice - a habit of which we may easily assume Ben Elton to disapprove. This is especially bizarre, when Agnes goes on to say: "'If only you had been a coward.'" Why give him the white feather then?

The character of Abercrombie, introduced in Chapter four is, again, rather 'Sassoonish': a homosexual poet, who has been awarded a medal for bravery. The main difference between the two characters is that Sassoon would not have been so crude or obvious and this is where we see the pen of Ben Elton at work, as we are offered a larger than life character in creation. At the same time though, Abercrombie doesn't feel real: there is something of the thigh-slapping pantomime personality about him, which seems incongruous. Personally, I wonder whether Ben Elton put less effort into the creation of this character because he knew he was going to kill him off.

In Chapter five, we have yet another scene change and, I have to say, these can become rather distracting and confusing, especially in this first section of the novel. We are introduced to Hopkins, because he will play a pivotal role later on, but also because we are supposed to compare his character to that of Kingsley. Neither will give way in a matter of principle and both firmly believe that they are always right. The comparison, however, is rather too obvious and contrived to be taken seriously. Ben Elton doubtless wishes us to sympathise with Hopkins, who represents not only the working class, but also the 'poor bloody infantry'. There is also a contrast to be drawn between the camaraderie displayed between the ranking soldiers portrayed here and the upper-class officers shown in the previous chapter.

CHAPTERS 6-10

Chapter 6

In prison, Kingsley, having been sentenced to two years hard labour, is being taken to see the governor. No-one within the prison welcomes his arrival: his fellow inmates know his as a policeman; the warders as a shirker; the governor believes Kingsley to be a traitor. The atmosphere that surrounds him is dangerous, as Kingsley soon realises that there will be no protection from abuse while he remains incarcerated. Nonetheless, during his interview with the governor, Kingsley sticks to his guns, causing the governor, whose son had been killed at Loos, to become extremely angry.

Chapter 7

Abercrombie, Stamford and the rest of the officers are enjoying a welcome dinner behind the lines. The cooks and servants have procured a feast, which the officers all consume before the colonel makes a long speech, welcoming all the new officers to the Regiment. He makes a special mention of Abercrombie, whose poetry and bravery he much admires. After the meal, Stamford contrives to go for a walk with Abercrombie and reveals that he loves the Viscount, which confession is cruelly rebuffed. Abercrombie reminds Stamford that whatever may have happened between them in London is now irrelevant. Stamford is devastated, but Abercrombie is unmoved and adamant that he feels nothing for the younger man.

Later, when alone, Abercrombie tries to write to the mother of one of his fellow officers, who had died some time before. This officer, named Merivale had, it transpires, been Abercrombie's lover and the two men had formed an extremely close bond, akin to conventional marriage. It is clear that whatever Abercrombie may have said to Stamford about the impossibility of two men having a close relationship, that is not the real reason behind his own reluctance to show affection to Stamford.

Chapter 8

In prison, Kingsley faces his first meal and his primary problem is being served, as the man who dishes out the food refuses to serve him. When Kingsley suggests serving himself, the warder punches him, before asking if any of the assembled crowd will serve 'the traitor'. Just as it seems that no-one will, a man named McAlistair steps forward and offers. McAlistair is a union leader and makes his offer in defence of Kingsley's human rights. However, when Kingsley asks permission to eat with McAlistair, he is treated to a tirade of abuse. This episode makes Kingsley realise that he has no friends and that his influence and opinions count for nothing.

Chapter 9

Later, after his meal, Kingsley is taken to his cell by Senior Warder Jenkins, who had once been a sergeant serving under Kingsley in the Metropolitan Police. However, Kingsley had found it necessary to dismiss him. Inside the cell, Kingsley finds himself sharing his living space with three men for whose incarceration he is responsible. Within moments, the three men have set upon him, beating him unconscious.

Chapter 10

In his first duty in charge of his new company, Abercrombie must mete out the punishment to Private Hopkins. Although Abercrombie is new and unfamiliar with either Hopkins or his offence, he tries to be fair but firm in his handling of the situation. Hopkins, however, is undeterred and hurls abuse at Abercrombie before being given Field Punishment Number One, which involves being tied to a gun carriage wheel for a day.

Critical Appraisal of Chapters 6-10

Chapter six places us back in the prison where Kingsley is placed in amongst the hardened criminals at Wormwood Scrubs. This course of action would have been almost unheard of, as most imprisoned conscientious objectors were kept isolated and in silence - this was deemed to be one of their punishments. Ben Elton clearly wishes to create a malicious and dangerous environment, devoid of comfort or hope, which the reader may compare unfavourably with life at the front. However, it is again rather convenient that the governor of the prison should have a son who died a hero's death and also that the warder should be portrayed as a chirpy cockney as these are both such stereotypes.

The welcome meal devoured by Abercrombie and his fellow officers in the next chapter goes to prove another commonly-held theory: that the officers dined in lavish style, while the men struggled by on meagre rations. The remainder of chapter seven begins to demonstrate Abercrombie as a neurotic: he writes to the mother of his dead lover, while treating the living with contempt. Stamford, meanwhile, is being portrayed being portrayed as a hapless, love-lorn wimp, although even now the reader is able to sense that his role will be more important than that. The plot is now undisguised. It is blindingly obvious that Abercrombie will be the murder victim, although the problem here is that the reader doesn't really care about him, because he is such a stereotype. We neither love, nor loathe him, so we are not really very interested in finding out what happens next.

In Chapter eight, we have moved back into the prison again and the only purpose I can see for including this chapter at all is to allow McAlistair's character to have a rant at Kingsley. Of course, we learn more about the harsh environment of the prison, but we have already heard about this before and we will hear more about it in the ensuing chapters, so it's all a bit dull. In addition, however, we do learn that Kingsley is not very bright. Just because McAlistair offers to serve him his food, doesn't mean he wants to sit and eat with him, and what on earth would make Kingsley think otherwise?

The introduction of Senior Warder Jenkins in Chapter nine signifies yet another 'convenience', as he had previously worked with Kingsley, but his work had been so unsatisfactory that he had been discharged from the police force - a situation for which he naturally holds Kingsley responsible. This man, Jenkins, then 'conveniently' arranges that Kingsley's cell-mates are men for whose incarceration Kingsley is responsible. The list of unashamed coincidences here is quite ridiculous, to the point where the reader is simply anticipating the next ludicrous twist.

Within the context of these coincidences and, given the storyline that is to follow, it is not surprising that Abercrombie should be the officer responsible for punishing Hopkins. Ben Elton has written this passage as though he agrees with Hopkins's position and feels that Field Punishment Number One is barbaric. Looking at it from the relative comfort of the early 21st century, it may well seem so. However, all soldiers at the time would have been aware of the penalties for misdemeanours and would, therefore, have little cause for complaint.

CHAPTERS 11-15

Chapter 11

Kingsley is admitted to the prison hospital, where the doctor informs Jenkins that the patient is sufficiently damaged to warrant several days of rest and observation. Although Jenkins initially objects to this, the doctor reminds him that Kingsley's untimely death would be detrimental and that any ensuing enquiry might cause problems. Jenkins reluctantly agrees to Kingsley remaining in the hospital and he and the doctor leave Kingsley in the care of an Irish orderly who immediately offers Kingsley some morphine, which is declined. However, the orderly takes the morphine himself and writes down in the notes that he gave it to Kingsley, asking the policeman to keep quiet about this deception. Later, while the orderly sleeps, Kingsley wonders whether he might be able to form an alliance with any other prisoners or groups of prisoners, who might be willing to offer him protection.

When the orderly awakes, Kingsley asks him whether there are any members of the Irish Republican Brotherhood in the prison and, although the orderly is doubtful that they would be prepared to form an alliance, he seems willing to arrange a meeting.

Chapter 12

It is dawn on the morning of 31st July 1917 and Abercrombie and his men are in the front line trenches, awaiting the beginning of the Third Battle of Ypres [also known as Passchendaele]. Unlike on previous similar occasions, Abercrombie is extremely apprehensive about this particular assault and struggles to keep his nerves under control. He worries that he will not be able to give the order to go over the top and will, therefore, blacken his previously good reputation. He recalls that during the night, he had seen Stamford and that the two men had shaken hands and exchanged a comforting, friendly glance, before parting.

Chapter 13

On the evening of 31st July, Abercrombie, having done his duty and taken his men into battle, now finds that he is mute. A slight wound necessitates a visit to a field dressing station, where Abercrombie also informs the doctor of his inability to speak, whereupon he is sent further back down the line to the Royal Army Medical Corps operating centre. Here, he joins a group of similarly troubled men, among whom is Private Hopkins. The Colonel is surprised by this turn of events and wonders how Abercrombie will react to the discovery that he has been broken. Another doctor asks the Colonel if he will forward Abercrombie's papers, as the Viscount has made an 'insistent' request for them.

Chapter 14

By now, Kingsley has been in hospital for almost a week and is beginning to despair of any assistance from the Irish Republican Brotherhood. However, one night, he is visited by three men who offer him protection in return for information. Unfortunately, the information they require is the names of Irish informants, working for the British Secret Service and Kingsley is unwilling to betray these men, as he knows that his betrayal will lead to their deaths. The Irishmen leave him, despite his pleas for help.

Chapter 15

In a chateau at Merville in France, many victims of shell shock are gathered together, trying to sleep despite their varied and terrible nightmares. Among them are Hopkins and two others, who lie together 'in a lovers' embrace'. Later on, there is a shot, although no-one seems to notice.

Critical Appraisal of Chapters 11-15

The inclusion of the Irish Republican Brotherhood enables Ben Elton to mention another controversial event in British military history, namely the Irish Rebellion or Easter Rising as it was also known, which took place in April 1916. It must be said that some members of Sinn Fein, who had been imprisoned after the Easter Rising, were sympathetic towards conscientious objectors, although it does sometimes feel in this novel as though Ben Elton has a desire to include as much military, social and political history as possible, some of which is not entirely necessary to the plot itself.

Chapter twelve finds us in the front line trenches, awaiting the moment of attack and now we are given a portrait of Abercrombie as a fading hero, which belies the thigh-slapping caricature of previous scenes. We are told that his nervous reaction is not 'uncommon amongst men who have seen a year or two of constant service', which is quite true; except that Abercrombie has not been in 'constant' service, since he has only just returned from leave. 'Constant' service would be where a man is repeatedly declined leave, for whatever reason. Also, up until now, Abercrombie really hasn't been portrayed as the nervous type and yet this is clearly the path down which we are now being steered. In addition, Abercrombie is evidently worried about being able to give the order to his men and that he would be 'disgraced' for failing to do so. Such a train of thought seems bizarre for a man who has by now taken to writing anti-war poetry and who is presumably already contemplating resigning his commission.

The obvious result of Abercrombie's nerves is shell-shock, which shows itself in this instance, by the patient becoming mute. I think it would have been more interesting and realistic if Abercrombie and Hopkins could have displayed different symptoms. However, the real problem here lies with the fact that we are given no details: there is no explanation for either man's shell-shock; we are just supposed to believe in it. The ensuing passages between the medical officer and the colonel are loaded with irony and satire, which could have been used to much better effect, giving the reader a more thorough understanding of Abercrombie and the reasons behind his breakdown, instead of which we are treated to a tirade of political commentaries regarding the lack of military understanding about shell-shock and the insensitivity of the higher ranks, who, it would seem, would prefer to be shooting grouse, to shooting Germans. Maybe there wasn't enough sympathy at the time towards those who suffered from neurosis (although by 1917, advances has been made), but this is a novel and we want to know more about the characters involved, not be lectured on the shortcomings, or otherwise, of the British Army or its leaders.

Chapter fourteen begins with another of several infuriating time references: 'On the evening that... ', which continue for the next few chapters, becoming increasingly distracting and repetitive. By the following chapter, however, the murder has taken place. With no witnesses to the shot, which happens amid the confusion of so many neurotic patients, it would appear that it is going to be difficult to prove anything. As such, the scene is being set, rather obviously, for our hero Kingsley, to perform miracles.

CHAPTERS 16-20

Chapter 16

At the Carlton Club in London, Lord Abercrombie receives news of his son's death from an undersecretary of the Home Office, who states that Captain Abercrombie died at the Battle of Ypres. Lord Abercrombie is stunned - not so much by the news of his son's death, but by the fact that the army has stated that he died in battle. This he states to be impossible, because he spoke to his son on the telephone the night before from the Chateau in France. Thus begins the mystery and intrigue surrounding Captain Abercrombie's death.

Chapter 17

In the prison hospital, Kingsley has managed to convince the doctor, who is a drunkard, that he has several broken ribs and, therefore, the doctor insists that Kingsley must be kept in the hospital even longer, much to Jenkins's disgust.

Chapter 18

At the Carlton Club, Lord Abercrombie is informed by the Secretary of State for War, that Captain Abercrombie was murdered. Lord Abercrombie is, initially, incredulous, but when it is explained that the man who killed his son is a Bolshevik, he begins to understand. He agrees to keep the manner of his son's death a secret for the good of the nation and to preserve Viscount Abercrombie's reputation. He is, however, adamant that the man responsible must be executed.

Chapter 19

In the sitting room of Fabians Sidney and Beatrice Webb, sit several prominent socialists, including the politicians Ramsay MacDonald and Arthur Henderson. Between them, they argue heatedly over the fate of Private Hopkins, who seems to have disappeared. They agree that the army should come clean about what happened and that justice should be done, failing which they will publish the information which they have regarding Abercrombie's death.

Chapter 20

After another week in hospital, Kingsley is awoken by the arrival of a different orderly who explains, mysteriously, that Kingsley can escape and that he will arrange for strategic doors to be left unlocked. That night, acting on this man's instructions, Kingsley effects his escape, only to find himself in the prison courtyard, surrounded by armed guards. They want him to run, so that they can shoot him, while trying to escape. Although Kingsley quickly realises that he has been set up and refuses to move, the man in charge shoots him anyway.

Critical Appraisal of Chapters 16-20

Although the reader is aware of an intriguing 'shot in the dark', the author needs to create an air of mystery surrounding the death of Captain Abercrombie, since one more corpse in the middle of a war is hardly likely to raise many eyebrows. His method of doing this is to definitely place Abercrombie in France, rather than Ypres, by having him telephone his parents on the evening before his death. While telecommunications may well have been fairly advanced in 1917, I have never heard of an army officer being permitted to telephone his family. If that were the case, what would be the point in censorship? Officers and men could simply pick up the nearest telephone and tell their loved ones where they were and what they were doing. Communications - even between Generals and their families - took place by letter or telegram. However, these methods would not suit the author's purpose, since the former would take too long to arrive and the latter might have been sent by anyone. Nonetheless, a little realism might be nice and I am sure that Lord Abercrombie's point could have been made in some other way.

Lord Abercrombie's subsequent acquiescence in the cover-up of his son's murder seems somewhat bizarre, given his initial reaction, but once again, as a character does a complete u-turn, the reader is given little explanation and is expected to simply accept the situation because it suits the plot.

The same could be said to apply to the introduction of the Fabians in chapter nineteen. Beatrice and Sidney Webb were indeed renowned for their political soirees, but here their inclusion feels contrived, and seems to be here just to allow Ben Elton to demonstrate the depth of his political knowledge, rather than adding anything significant to the plot.

The manner of Kingsley's escape, the fact of which has been obvious since the moment of Abercrombie's murder, is ridiculous considering everything that has gone before. The warders, especially Jenkins, would surely have been queuing up to pull the trigger, rather than allowing a complete stranger the privilege. While we are clearly supposed to believe that Captain Shannon is diabolically good at his job, it does seem quite hard to believe that this prison break-out could go off without a single hitch, especially when Kingsley himself has not a clue what is happening.

CHAPTERS 21-25

Chapter 21

Agnes Kingsley - or Beaumont as she is now calling herself - is visited by Captain Shannon who works for Army Intelligence. He informs Agnes that her husband has been shot while trying to escape from prison. She is genuinely devastated and just before Shannon departs, she asks him to call her Mrs Kingsley.

Chapter 22

Kingsley who, much to his own surprise, is still very much alive, is in the back of a car with Captain Shannon and another man. He is blindfolded and has no idea where he is being taken, or why and even when he joins in the conversation, he learns little more, other then the fact that it was Shannon who shot him using a rubber bullet and that Agnes has been informed of his 'death'. It would seem that the army have some purpose for him, but they are not about to give him any details as yet.

Chapter 23

As bleak, curt messages of sympathy begin to arrive at the Kingsley home, Agnes realises how much she still loves her husband, despite her protests to the contrary, and how much is now lost to her forever.

Chapter 24

Kingsley wakes in a Folkestone hotel, with Captain Shannon. After a bath and a change of clothes, the two men go for a walk. They watch a Pierrot show on the promenade and Shannon is rude to the performers. Afterwards, Kingsley threatens to disappear unless Shannon explains what is going on, but he is persuaded to have brunch first.

Chapter 25

Agnes Kingsley attends her husband's funeral at Wormwood Scrubs, although Shannon had informed Kingsley that she would not. The funeral is a very rushed affair and it would seem that everyone wants Kingsley out of the way and forgotten as soon as possible.

Critical Appraisal of Chapters 21-25

The meeting between Agnes Kingsley and Captain Shannon provides us with our first introduction to the S.I.S. man and here he is portrayed as 'genuinely sympathetic' and self deprecating. However, by the very next chapter, we already begin to see the flaws in Shannon's character, which is too soon for my liking and makes his role fairly obvious, even from this early stage. The whole point of a 'whodunit' murder mystery is that the reader should be left guessing, whereas here, Shannon is so obviously shady, that his ultimate part in the plot is transparent. However, to be fair, it is only really with the introduction of Shannon's character that the story begins to get interesting. Although the course of action has been fairly obvious, it is better now that it is actually under way.

Shannon's character, however, quickly degenerates into the comic cad or bounder of Victorian melodrama. His personality is imposed, rather than explained to the reader and, therefore, it doesn't really work or make sense.

CHAPTERS 26-30

Chapter 26

Over brunch at the Majestic Hotel, Shannon explains to Kingsley why he has been released from prison in such an elaborate, secretive fashion: the government wants him to investigate the death of Viscount Abercrombie. Kingsley is unsure about accepting this commission, but Shannon tells him that a meeting has been arranged in London for the following day and that Kingsley should at least listen to what is being asked of him. In the meantime, however, Shannon is keen to spend the remainder of his day in Folkestone, with a young waitress named Violet and, therefore, arranges that Kingsley will make his own way to London. This is a clear dereliction of duty, but Shannon is obviously only interested in pleasuring himself and, although Kingsley disapproves, he agrees to Shannon's plan. Before parting, the two men agree that Kingsley needs an alias and they settle on the name Christopher Marlowe.

Chapter 27

Left to his own devices, Kingsley decides to visit the public library in Folkestone, where he observes young families in mourning and compares their situations with that which he imagines must currently be being endured by Agnes and George, who believe him to be dead. He tries, unsuccessfully to write a letter to Agnes and then decides instead to read the newspaper reports on Viscount Abercrombie's death. The local newspaper, which is available, reports that Abercrombie was killed in action and then goes on to give a brief history of his life and war record, before quoting his popular poem 'Forever England' which Kingsley dislikes.

Finding nothing else of interest regarding Abercrombie, Kingsley begins to contemplate Captain Shannon, whose role in the case he finds dubious. Kingsley also worries about Violet and, seemingly resolved upon some immediate course of action, he quickly leaves the library.

Chapter 28

Having bedded one of the 'Pierrette' actresses, the insatiable Shannon meets with Violet and takes her on a bus ride to an isolated spot on the beach. Here, he attempts to kiss her, but when Violet resists, Shannon becomes violent, forcing himself on her. Luckily for Violet, Kingsley arrives just in time and Shannon is persuaded to allow the young girl to leave unmolested.

Chapter 29

Shannon and Kingsley part company once more and Kingsley makes his way back to the library to while away the few hours that remain to him, before his train departs for London. Suddenly, he hears the sounds of droning overhead, which signals an attack of 'Gothas' or German bombers. An air-raid follows and, among the casualties whom he tries to assist, Kingsley finds one of the children that he had earlier observed in the library, bleeding to death in her mother's arms.

Chapter 30

Back in London, Kingsley finds himself at his old home, desirous only to see Agnes and George once more, although he knows that he cannot make himself known to them. He watches Agnes through the drawing room window, noting how uncharacteristically melancholy she is. Then he takes an enormous risk and climbs up to his son's bedroom, where he watches George sleeping. Before long, however, Kingsley hears Agnes approaching and is forced to hide, observing her confusion regarding the now-open window and curtains. Agnes talks to the sleepy George and then to herself, revealing how much she misses her husband and Kingsley is overwhelmed with joy that his marriage might not be entirely lost to him after all. Before departing, he vows quietly to his still-sleeping son, that he will return one day.

Critical Appraisal of Chapters 26-30

Shannon's character rapidly deteriorates into a complete womaniser. However, there are problems here, since his fall, in the eyes of the reader at least, is so rapid that it defies belief and also in that his vocabulary and actions are so melodramatic and cliched that one half expects him to be wearing a cape and twirling dark moustaches, while referring to all women as 'comely wenches'. His portrayal is, therefore, too extreme and too obviously mad, bad and dangerous to be taken seriously.

The interlude which Kingsley spends in the library is, presumably, included to give Shannon time to molest his way around Folkestone, but also to show the reader the more serious, policeman side to Kingsley's character who, at the first opportunity, decides to begin work on the investigation. It does, however, take him quite some while to realise Shannon's 'wicked' intentions with regard to Violet, which is slightly worrying for a man with such a superior intellect. One wonders whether Ben Elton thought this delay might add to the tension surrounding Violet's fate, but if so, I'm afraid it did not work.

The whole situation surrounding Violet is clearly designed to flesh out the characters of Shannon and Kingsley: to show that Shannon is amoral and that Kingsley will always do what is right. However, the author has turned this scene into a melodrama of lavish proportions, with cliched language and actions, while the reader feels so assured of Violet's rescue that the whole incident is wasted. It is very hard to believe that a hardened Metropolitan policeman, trying to prevent a rape is going to say: 'Unhand that girl'. I would have been much more convinced by more coarse language, or even direct action on Kingsley's part. Why couldn't he drag Shannon off the young helpless girl and give him a good thrashing? The rape scene itself is not much better, simply because it is too coy. There is too much ranting from Shannon about a soldier's right to 'comfort' - of all things - and not enough action. Although it is excessively unpleasant, in a fictional rape scene, the reader ought to at least feel some of the fear of the victim, otherwise there is little point in having a molestation in the first place. Here, not only does the reader feel assured of Violet's rescue at all times but, because there is insufficient detail, we cannot understand her fear and, therefore, we don't really care about what happens to her.

The ensuing air raid is another situation which smacks of trying to get a little bit of everything into the story. However, it really serves no purpose whatsoever and, in terms of the plot, we could easily move straight from chapter twenty-eight to chapter thirty. The death of the little girl has an element of Schindler's List about it [In the film, Oskar Schindler witnesses the Nazi clearance of the Jewish ghettos and sees a little girl in a red coat whom he thinks has escaped their clutches. Later, he spots her body on a funeral pyre.] Presumably, we are supposed to believe that this is some kind of revelation for Kingsley: a moment when he is emotionally touched by the war to a point which changes his perspective.

In chapter thirty, we learn of yet another side to Kingsley's character, as this man who had been prepared to sacrifice his wife and child for the sake of a principle is now portrayed as the perfect husband and father. We discover that he was always rushing home from work, armed with flowers and chocolates or cakes to spend happy evenings in the warm embrace of his family. It seems ridiculous that this man would sacrifice so much for a principle - or at least, it does when we have been told so little about the reasons behind his protest and arrest. It makes no sense for the character that is being portrayed here to have acted in this manner, considering the great sacrifices he would have been making. Without more detail as to his protest, this whole aspect of the novel seems nonsensical.

CHAPTERS 31-35

Chapter 31

After breakfast, Kingsley makes his way to his pre-arranged meeting with Captain Shannon. En-route, he comes upon a meeting of communist and pacifist speakers in Trafalgar Square. Among these is Bertrand Russell, who mentions Kingsley by name, as a heroic conscientious objector. Kingsley, although still well disguised and unrecognisable, is handed a white feather by a young girl - not because she knows who he is, but because he is not in uniform. As the crowd becomes more boisterous and Kingsley hears the approach of policemen, he continues on his way, anxious to escape any unwanted attention. Near Downing Street, Kingsley passes Winston Churchill, in conversation with Admiral Jellicoe and then eventually meets up with Captain Shannon, who, it transpires has been following him all morning. Shannon shows Kingsley where he needs to go and leaves him to attend the meeting alone.

Chapter 32

Kingsley has a meeting with Sir Mansfield Cumming, chief of the Secret Intelligence Service, at which he discovers that his mission is to travel to France to investigate the murder of Captain Abercrombie. The authorities are, it would seem, not convinced that Hopkins is the guilty party, even though the military police have arrested him. Politically, it has become necessary that someone neutral, as well as capable, should investigate this crime, and this is why Kingsley has been released from prison. It would seem that two witnesses observed an officer near Abercrombie's room at around the time of his murder: one is a man named McCroon who is a political ally of Hopkins's and is deemed unreliable. The other is a nurse and she would seem to represent Kingsley's best lead in his investigation. Kingsley is informed that upon the conclusion of the case, he would be expected to emigrate. Right at the end of their conversation, the two men are interrupted by the arrival of the Prime Minister, David Lloyd George.

Chapter 33

Lloyd George and his secretary, Miss Thompson, enter the room, although the latter is very shortly dismissed again, since the matter under discussion is so sensitive. The Prime Minister explains again the seriousness of the situation and

Kingsley agrees that he will help, whereupon Lloyd George leaves. Kingsley is then kitted out with the uniform of a Captain in the Military Police and he and Sir Mansfield go to lunch.

Chapter 34

Despite Cumming's initial concerns, Kingsley suggests that they test his disguise by lunching at his favourite restaurant, Simpsons-in-the-Strand, to which Cumming reluctantly agrees. En-route they are joined by Captain Shannon and it is clear that Cumming holds him in the same low regard as Kingsley. Over a fine lunch, Kingsley questions Shannon regarding the evidence of Nurse Murray and Private McCroon. It would seem that Shannon has made himself very familiar with Nurse Murray, although Cumming seems blissfully unaware of the Captain's methods. Once Cumming has left, Shannon informs Kingsley that he should avoid contacting his family again. He also reveals that he has met Agnes Kingsley and makes several lewd insinuations about her which cause Kingsley to threaten Shannon. The two men arrange to meet later, so that Shannon can give Kingsley his papers in preparation for his departure for France.

Chapter 35

Kingsley goes to watch a music hall show, but leaves when they begin to play a song that he and Agnes had particularly enjoyed. At the railway station, he meets Shannon and receives his documents and travel instructions. Shannon then departs with a nurse who he met earlier in the day. Kingsley's boat crossing is long and uncomfortable, but eventually, he lands in France and finds himself in a train facing another long and arduous journey. He chooses to divest himself of his rank badges and mixes with the ordinary soldiers, rather than the officers.

Critical Appraisal of Chapters 31-35

Chapter thirty-one is another pointless chapter, which could easily have been omitted. Kingsley could have simply arrived at his meeting, without all this rigmarole in between. This chapter involves a lot of historical and political name dropping, presumably to prove that the author has done some research. However, what are the chances of coming across Bertrand Russell, Winston Churchill and Admiral Jellicoe, all in the space of a few minutes? This seems more than a little far fetched and, again it smacks of trying to cram in as much of the war as possible, since in this one chapter there are references to pacifists, white feathers, the Dardanelles, the above mentioned personalities, protest meetings, politics and so on.

As Kingsley enters into his meeting with Cumming, the plot becomes even more contrived. It does seem a little unrealistic to suppose that no-one would have really looked into the death of Abercrombie properly in the first place. In addition, Kingsley's intelligence is again called into question, as he wonders 'why they needed him', when it has been blindingly obvious to the reader since Abercrombie's death was first mentioned. As for having Lloyd George suddenly appear, this scene becomes nothing short of farcical, especially when he utters the immortal lines: 'I bloody 'ope not anyway, boyo! Do you see?' Again, however, this setting allows Ben Elton to drop names and historical facts into the story, demonstrating his knowledge, although these add nothing to the story and actually interrupt the plot entirely.

Lunch at Simpsons seems to have been arranged to remind us that, on the home front, relative luxury and abundance continue unabated, despite the war and this chapter is written with an air of distaste, as we are told that Cumming talks 'through his roast beef'.

During his journey, although Kingsley might be able to cast off his 'red tabs' and military police insignia, he would still appear to be an officer as his uniform itself would be different to that of the enlisted men. Therefore, the idea of him throwing 'his lot' in with them and being referred to as their 'mate' or 'pal' is unrealistic and improbable.

CHAPTERS 36-40

Chapter 36

During one of its interminable stops, the men leave the train and take the opportunity to defecate. Kingsley is initially uncertain about going to the toilet so publicly, but soon manages to join in. A conversation develops between the men about the origins of the war and a very well-versed corporal explains to the others how the treaty system came to cause the conflict. Another man disagrees and spouts some communist rhetoric, which the others soon decry. Before long, they are recalled to the train, but Kingsley takes the opportunity to ask the communist's opinion of Abercrombie's death and, it would seem that it is fairly widely known that the Viscount did not die in battle.

Chapter 37

Upon arrival at their destination, Kingsley leaves the train and gets a lift to the Chateau in the back of an ambulance, in which all of the patients seem to be suffering from shell-shock. This provides Kingsley with a most disturbing and uncomfortable ride. When he gets to the chateau, Kingsley begins to look around and, while watching two men ineffectually kicking a football, he is joined by Nurse Murray. She immediately makes her opinions very clear; one of which is that she hates policemen of every type, with a 'passion'. Undeterred, Kingsley suggests a walk and questions Nurse Murray regarding the night of Abercrombie's death. She is adamant that she saw a 'furtive' British officer leaving Abercrombie's room and she is equally certain of Hopkins's innocence. She recalls the night of the crime; the military policemen's' treatment of Hopkins and their inefficiency in death with the scene of the crime.

Nurse Murray makes it clear that no proper investigation or autopsy was carried out, which astounds Kingsley. They briefly discuss Captain Shannon and Kingsley is clearly embarrassed by Nurse Murray's 'outspoken' references to her sexual relationship with Shannon. She also tells him about a poetry group which she organises at the hospital to help the men, although she, like Kingsley, thought little of Abercrombie's verses. Nurse Murray reveals that Abercrombie had requested a 'green envelope' and, although Kingsley has no idea of the significance of this, he must remain in ignorance of this for the time being.

Later, the couple return to the chateau and Nurse Murray shows Kingsley the room in which Abercrombie had been staying. It is now occupied by another man, who seems to do nothing but masturbate and he continues in this practice, while Kingsley and Nurse Murray carry on their conversation. Among Abercrombie's personal effects, it transpires that there had been no documents and that one of his boots had gone missing. Kingsley seems to find these pieces of information to be of great interest. They then pass on to McCroon's room, although McCroon himself has returned to his regiment. Finally, Murray offers Kingsley a cup of tea and they return to her billet in the servants' quarters. While she brews the tea, he enquires why she dislikes the police so much and discovers that she is a suffragette and, before the war was arrested many times.

Chapter 38

Later, Kingsley goes to find his billet, which is above an estaminet in Merville. Having washed, he orders food and, while eating, he is joined by some men from Abercrombie's regiment, who soon start to discuss the Viscount's death. Kingsley has removed his insignia again, so the men talk quite freely and seem to be mainly of the opinion that Hopkins would not have shot Abercrombie. Finally, Kingsley departs, having first revealed his real rank and position to the shocked audience.

Chapter 39

That evening, Kingsley 'accompanies' Nurse Murray to a concert at the hospital. Among the performers is a drag act, which includes Lieutenant Stamford. After the show, Nurse Murray introduces Kingsley to Stamford and they briefly discuss the lieutenant's performance, before Nurse Murray turns the conversation in the direction of Abercrombie's death. Stamford remains adamant that Abercrombie died in battle, although it is clear that he knows differently since he admits to having spent most of the afternoon of his death with the Viscount. Stamford has been writing poetry and leaves a few examples with Nurse Murray for her to read, before departing.

She is then accosted by other officers, so after interviewing a few men, Kingsley decides to head back to his billet. He hasn't gone far, however, when Nurse Murray catches him up. She asserts that Hopkins did not murder Abercrombie and, although she can give no evidence for this, she is sure of his innocence. In the darkness, Murray and Kingsley are unable to progress further and, as it starts to rain more heavily, they shelter under the trees. Nurse Murray seems unsure that Kingsley is what he claims to be and is doubtful about all of the events surrounding Abercrombie's death: following Shannon's arrival, Abercrombie had been murdered, then Hopkins arrested and then Kingsley had appeared. She reveals that she has seen through at least part of his disguise, in that he doesn't behave like a military policeman and clearly has no idea what green envelopes are used for. Kingsley has no reply to this, so Nurse Murray explains that the purpose of a green envelope is that the contents will not be censored. Usually, she says, the men use them to send home letters about 'sex and moaning'. Having established that Kingsley is not a soldier, he reveals that he is, nonetheless, a policeman.

Despite her disappointment, Nurse Murray becomes more friendly and allows Kingsley to call her by her Christian name: Kitty. As the rain falls harder, Kingsley offers Kitty his coat and during the process of handing this over, Kitty contrives to place Kingsley's hand on her breast, inside her now-unbuttoned blouse. Without really thinking, Kingsley begins to kiss her, but then stops abruptly, revealing that he is married and loves his wife. Kitty seems unperturbed by this revelation and kneels down in front of Kingsley. Despite his misgivings, Kingsley is easily persuaded to have sex with Kitty. Afterwards, she reveals that her relationship with Captain Shannon had ended badly, but she and Kingsley agree to remain friends, although she obviously knows that Christopher Marlowe is not his real name. Once Kitty has departed, Kingsley is overcome by feelings of guilt.

Chapter 40

The next day, Kingsley goes to the Military Police station at Armentieres, where he looks over the inadequate records of the case and interviews Private Hopkins, who informs him that he overheard Abercrombie arguing with somebody shortly before his death. Kingsley issues instructions that Abercrombie's body is to be exhumed and also discovers that both McCroon and the murder weapon have been returned to the front line. Having established the whereabouts of the gun, Kingsley decides to pursue it personally, leaving McCroon and the exhumation to one side for the time being.

Critical Appraisal of Chapters 36-40

Chapter thirty-six provides yet another pointless episode. It demonstrates that the author has a broad understanding of the causes of the First World War, but this is supposed to be a story, not a history book. One also has to question whether any benefit is really to be gained from the toilet break itself, other than that it proves the point of one critic (Jane Jakeman, writing in The Independent), who comments aptly on Ben 'Elton's usual obsessions with defecation and masturbation, interspersed with undigested information'. If it is really necessary, which in my view it isn't, for us to have a banal history lesson, then why could this not take place in the carriage of the train? Nothing is gained from either the 'toilet' humour or the historical references and, if anything, they detract from the story.

The introduction of Nurse Kitty Murray gives us a further stereotypical character to add to our ever-increasing list, for here we have the jolly, pretty, 'gung-ho' suffragette who, needless to say, has to hate policemen. She is extremely frank and open in her speech, but this allows us to see yet another side of Kingsley's personality as he quickly becomes tongue-tied and embarrassed. Again, it seems as though Ben Elton is keen to cram another historical aspect into his novel - this time it is the Women's Suffrage Movement. Within this chapter, he also adds the treatment of shell-shock victims and the hunger strikes, release and re-arrest of Suffragettes under the Cat and Mouse Act of 1913. In a final clumsiness, for this chapter at least, Ben Elton has Kingsley looking back over all the times that his conscience has failed him in the past. By this stage, the novel is knee-deep in historical and political versifying to a point where it feels almost as bogged down as the mud of Flanders itself.

Chapter thirty-eight sees Kingsley indulging in a very uncharacteristic and unwise piece of schoolboy one-upmanship, when he reveals his position to the men assembled in the estaminet. This seems bizarre, considering that he has gone to some efforts to conceal his identity, but also when one bears in mind that he is in the very early stages of his investigation and, therefore, continued anonymity amongst these men might well prove advantageous. Considering Kingsley's supposedly superior intelligence, this rather amateur 'reveal' seems uncharacteristically stupid.

The development of the relationship between Kingsley and Kitty Murray is extremely rapid, to say the least. Within the space of a few hours, we are supposed to accept that their characters have met, had a few brief conversations, almost entirely related to the murder enquiry, watched a concert and then had sex, which isn't bad, considering that one of them claims to be in love with someone else! It is difficult to accept that Kingsley, who had been so overcome with joy at the idea that Agnes missed him and had promised George that he would return home, could end up having sex with the first person who made him an offer.

The sex scene itself is also rather strange. Not only does Nurse Murray treat the whole exercise rather like a hunting spree with her 'golly', 'gosh', and 'tally-ho' exclamations, which are frankly unbelievable, but Ben Elton's language is so coy as to be laughable. It seems very peculiar that the author will go into vivid descriptions about the details of mens' toilet habits, but we are only told in very prim and Victorian terms of Kingsley's 'straining manhood'. Anyone who has read my study guides will know that I am not a great fan of unnecessary, gratuitous sex scenes in First World War literature. However, if we are to believe that Kingsley is going to commit adultery (and he will have sex with Kitty Murray again later in the story), then I'm afraid that we must understand why. This scene reads like something out of a bad romantic novel, which simply doesn't fit. If the author felt uncomfortable writing these scenes, it would have been better to have left them out altogether and allow the reader's imagination to do the work instead.

By this stage of the novel, the identity of the murderer has been made quite obvious, since we are told, very clearly, that Captain Shannon arrived at the chateau before Abercrombie's death, rather than as a result of it. The ensuing attempts to incriminate Stamford are, therefore, weakened, as is the plot, since the point of a murder mystery is that there should be some intrigue for the reader to enjoy.

CHAPTERS 41-45

Chapter 41

Slowly, Kingsley makes his way to Ypres, in pursuit of Captain Edmonds, who is now in possession of the murder weapon. Having eventually reached the rear lines, he then has to pass through networks of reserve, communication and support trenches. He stops to ask some men the whereabouts of Captain Edmonds and is informed that he is in the front line trenches. Almost as soon as Kingsley moves away, a shell lands in the traverse where he had just been standing, killing or wounding most of the men who had been there. Turning away from the sickening scene, Kingsley finally locates Captain Edmonds. Over a cup of onion-tasting tea, he explains that he needs to take Edmonds's gun away and has brought a replacement. Edmonds, however, is unwilling to allow Kingsley to take the pistol there and then, saying that he will have it sent back to Kingsley the next morning. When Kingsley protests, Edmonds explains that he is superstitious about his kit and is about to lead a raid that night and must take his existing weapon with him. Kingsley continues to remonstrate that Edmonds is being unreasonable, but the infantryman stands his ground. Aware that Edmonds may not return from the raid, Kingsley feels that he has no alternative but to follow him and his men on their assault.

Chapter 42

Kingsley slowly makes his way across No Man's Land, remaining to the rear of Edmonds and his raiding party, who soon reach the German barbed wire and begin to cut their way through. As Edmonds's men begin their assault on the German trench, Kingsley lies on top of the parapet above, observing, but not participating. All of a sudden, Edmonds is bayonetted and drops his revolver, so Kingsley jumps down into the trench using his replacement gun to defend himself. Having shot four men, Kingsley realises that Edmonds's guns is now nowhere to be seen. However, one of the victims of this gun is lying close by, so Kingsley uses a knife to remove a bullet from this corpse. By now the Germans are beginning to overrun the trench and Kingsley is most surprised to hear Edmonds, whom he had believed to be dead, telling him to get the men back to the British lines. Kingsley takes control, ordering one of the troopers to hand him a mills bomb [a popular name for a hand grenade], whereupon the two of them each hurl a grenade to either end of the trench, thereby buying time for Edmonds's men to withdraw, on Kingsley's command.

Edmonds urges Kingsley to leave him behind, but Kingsley will hear nothing of this, so he and the trooper manhandle Edmonds back over the parapet. Kingsley then manages to get Edmonds back to he British trenches where the young captain expresses his gratitude, before being carried away by stretcher bearers. Only then does Kingsley fully appreciate that, although his deeds may have been heroic, he has allowed himself to be drawn into the war and has killed many men - the very thing which he had sworn he would never do.

Chapter 43

Kingsley goes back down the line and visits Abercrombie's colonel at a nearby farmhouse, where he is treated to a hero's welcome. Not long after his arrival, Kingsley is joined by Private Cotton, Edmonds's batman [military name for a servant], who has followed the policeman and wishes to give him a slice of cake, in accordance with his captain's wishes. Kingsley and the colonel share the cake and some brandy, while the policeman questions the senior officer. The colonel had seen Abercrombie a couple of days after he arrived at the chateau and had taken his case of papers to him. As Kingsley leaves, the colonel says he will be recommending him for a medal.

Chapter 44

Kingsley travels back to Chateau Beaurivage, where he is surprisingly disappointed to discover that Nurse Murray is temporarily absent. The military police sergeant from Armentieres has performed the exhumation of Abercrombie's body and, upon close examination of the wound, Kingsley discovers fragments of rubber and leather, which lead him to the conclusion that Abercrombie must have been shot through the heel of his own boot, thus silencing the sound of the weapon. The boot would then have been discarded, which accounts for its absence. Kingsley removes the bullet from Abercrombie's brain and compares it to the one he took from the body of the German soldier in the trenches. He is shocked to discover that the two bullets do not match and could not, therefore, have been fired by the same gun. Kingsley concludes that Private Hopkins must be innocent and orders the sergeant to release him.

Chapter 45

Kingsley returns to the front line trenches in search of Private McCroon, whom he eventually finds with his company, about to go 'over the top'. Although Kingsley asks permission to take McCroon out of the line to interview him, the officer denies this and McCroon joins the attack, leaving Kingsley with little alternative in his own mind, other than to follow suit. Running across No Man's Land, Kingsley catches up with McCroon, only to discover that Hopkins is alongside him. Just as Kingsley realises the irony of this situation, however, Hopkins is blown to pieces by a German shell. Kingsley's feelings of guilt over Hopkins's death are ended abruptly by a second shell, which blows him and McCroon off their feet and into a nearby shell-hole. Once the two men are sufficiently recovered, Kingsley questions McCroon about the night of Abercrombie's death, when he had visited Hopkins in the chateau. McCroon is incredulous: Hopkins is dead, so what does it matter? Suddenly an officer appears and threatens to shoot them both if they do not rejoin the attack. Just as he seems likely to carry out his threat, however, his head is blown off, enabling Kingsley to continue his interrogation of McCroon. The private reveals that, contrary to earlier reports, he had seen an officer leave Abercrombie's room before Nurse Murray had left the ward and that he had been carrying a small leather case. Having gained this information, Kingsley makes his way back to the British lines.

Critical Appraisal of Chapters 41-45

Chapter forty-one starts well, as the author describes the initial parts of Kingsley's journey to the front line. However, these descriptions soon become turgid, as we are given a school text book style account of the trench system: 'fashioned in a zigzag pattern... to minimise the effect of the blast from a shell landing directly in a trench...' Fascinating facts, if facts are your main interest, but here we are concerned with a murder mystery, not the usefulness of the design of the British trench system, or the details as to how the men were rotated in and out of the front line. These unexciting explanations simply slow down a story which really needs to be moved along at a pace.

Then, one really has to question whether a military policeman - especially this particular military policeman - would go over the top on a raid for the sake of retrieving a piece of evidence. Kingsley claims to be of superior intelligence and if all he needs is a bullet, why does he not simply ask Captain Edmonds to discharge the gun and retrieve that bullet, rather than chasing him around No Man's Land. For a man with no fighting experience to go out in pursuit of a raiding party at night would not only endanger his own life and his investigation, but also the lives of all the other men participating in the raid. However, the raid is a more exciting scenario, and allows the author to put his hero in the position of having to break his bonds of conscience by killing the enemy, as well as rescue the survivors and the wounded Edmonds and, thereby save the day... Hurrah! The fact that the situation is unrealistic, impractical and out of character seems to be irrelevant.

The raid itself is fairly well described, but for me, it is not detailed enough. Considering that we have been given chapter and verse on the construction of the trench system, I would have liked to see much more detail included in scenes such as the raid itself. I want to know how Kingsley feels: is there fear, anticipation, excitement? It is night time, so how does he see what is going on? That is not made clear. As to his shooting of the enemy, there is more to follow on that subject in later chapters, but for now I will just say that if we are to believe that he is troubled by these deaths, then they should be dealt with in far greater depth and detail.

Having shot his enemies, Kingsley seems to have suddenly and miraculously developed a remarkable military knowledge, knowing exactly when and where to aim his Mills bombs and barking out orders like a seasoned professional - all of which seems extremely out of character, yet again, for a man who was prepared to sacrifice his beloved wife and son for his anti-war principles. However, his new-found military prowess does put him in the perfect position to turn the tables and find himself recommended for a medal, rather than being on the receiving end of a white feather.

The delivery of a nice slice of home-made cake simply tops off the whole affair, although being as Edmonds's company would still have been in the front line, much depleted after the raid and would have been expecting some kind of German counter-attack by way of reprisal, I find it very hard to believe that Private Cotton would have been permitted to wonder back behind the lines after Kingsley, to deliver the cake in the first place.

Next, the intrepid and multi-talented police inspector turns his hand to forensic science, examining the exhumed body of Captain Abercrombie; removing the bullet from his brain and comparing it with the one fired by Edmonds's gun. Without the assistance of any medical of scientific experts, Kingsley manages to conclude that, not only was Abercrombie shot through the heel of his boot, but also that Hopkins is innocent. The speed at which Kingsley reaches his conclusions is remarkable, as is his assurance that he must be right.

It seems absolutely ludicrous to me that Kingsley, who has evidently so greatly regretted his participation in the raid, should return so eagerly to the trenches. Then, that he would pursue McCroon over the top is senseless - he has little to gain, but everything to lose. Surely he wants to complete his investigation and return, as promised, to George? So why would he not wait in the trench, or make more of an effort to hold McCroon back? I find it very hard to believe that, considering the supposed importance of his mission, Kingsley would not have been given a Carte Blanche to allow him to effectively pull rank in such a situation. As for Ben Elton's assertion that Kingsley would be bothered by 'funk', or the appearance of fear - the man is a conscientious objector, or heaven's sake!

The timing and circumstances of Hopkins's death are too cliched to be believed. Almost the moment that Kingsley lays eyes on him, he is blown to pieces. However, only seconds earlier, McCroon had 'pulled his arm'. Are we actually supposed to believe that a blast which could make a man 'disintegrate', could leave another, just inches away, untouched? Of course, McCroon must be alive, for Kingsley to interview, but this version of Hopkins's demise is, frankly, preposterous.

CHAPTERS 46-50

Chapter 46

Kingsley makes his way back to the artillery lines where he sleeps, returning to Merville the next day. Upon arrival back at his billet, Kingsley is excited to discover that Nurse Murray is waiting in his room. After a brief discussion, which reveals that the 'colonel' who issued the military police with their initial orders does not exist, Kingsley removes his wet, soiled clothes. Kitty proceeds to sponge-bath Kingsley, while flirting, much to his embarrassment. With him now naked, Kitty undresses too, while they discuss the fate of Private Hopkins. They make love, despite Kingsley's guilt, but the next morning, she tries to assuage his remorse by explaining that the rules are different in war and she begs him not to tell his wife about his infidelity. Kingsley then explains that his wife has left him, and Kitty momentarily hopes that they could become a couple, before Kingsley explains that he still loves his wife, anyway. Kitty is clearly upset and Kingsley quickly realises that she has fallen in love with him, which makes him feel even more guilty. In order to hide her feelings, Kitty makes love to Kingsley again, after which, they discuss Stamford's poetry, which Kitty describes as 'angry' and 'intense'. The content of the poems makes Kingsley appreciate that Stamford could not possibly have written them.

Chapter 47

The next morning, after breakfast, Kingsley and Kitty return to the chateau, where they meet Stamford, who has recently been wounded. While Kitty changes her clothes, Kingsley interviews Stamford about his final meeting with Abercrombie and it soon becomes clear that Stamford is hiding something, especially concerning the leather case which he is carrying. Kitty reappears and discusses Stamford's poetry, questioning him on the style and content of his verses. Suddenly Kingsley interjects that the poems are not Stamford's, but are actually Abercrombie's. Stamford, thus exposed, tries to escape, although Kingsley easily catches up with him, whereupon Stamford explains that Abercrombie had asked him to destroy the poems. Having read them, however, Stamford had decided, following Abercrombie's death, to publish the poems as his own, partly for the fame which they might bring him and partly out of revenge, because Abercrombie had not loved him. Stamford explains that he and Abercrombie had argued on the night that Abercrombie was killed, but is adamant that he is not the murderer. Kingsley believes him, but Nurse Murray says she will keep Abercrombie's poems and burn them, as he had originally requested.

Chapter 48

Upon Stamford's departure, Kingsley sends a telegram to Sir Mansfield Cumming, explaining that an arrest is imminent. Next, he must go to the front lines again to re-interview Abercrombie's colonel. Nurse Murray offers to take him there on her motorcycle and they manage to get quite close to the lines before the machine can go no further. As Kingsley has to wait for the cover of darkness, Nurse Murray insists on waiting with him. They discuss the case, although Kingsley will not reveal who the murderer is. Kitty then discloses to a very embarrassed Kingsley that she is in love with him. He reiterates that he loves his wife and no-one else, despite Kitty's entreaties that they might be together. Kingsley feels guilty for causing Kitty so much pain. Having agreed to Kingsley's request that she should not burn Abercrombie's poems, Kitty leaves.

Chapter 49

As night falls, Kingsley joins an artillery observation officer, who is going in search of the 5th Battalion, East Lancashire Regiment. Eventually, they come across a runner who has been sent back by Colonel Hilton in search of water supplies. He explains that the 5th Battalion have made good progress, but have outflanked the troops on either side and are, therefore, exposed to the enemy. Kingsley and his companion progress forward, discovering a radio operator with a terrible abdominal wound. They are unable to give him water, but promise to send a stretcher party, although they both know that the man will soon be dead. All of a sudden, they encounter three German soldiers, but although both parties can clearly see each other, neither takes any action. Finally, they reach their objective, but just as they are about to enter the trench occupied by Colonel Hilton's men, they are caught by enemy machine-gun fire and Kingsley's companion, Philby, is wounded. This causes problems as, unable to report back their advanced position, it is quite likely that Hilton's men will soon come under fire from their own artillery. Hilton leaves a sergeant in charge and decides to go back himself to report the situation and get reinforcements, leaving Kingsley with little choice but to follow him across No Man's Land. Initially, they are forced to creep and crawl through the mud to avoid detection, but when they are almost back to the British lines, the German artillery opens fire and they have to take cover in a shell-hole.

Chapter 50

In their shell-hole, Kingsley and Colonel Hilton cower under an intense bombardment and, as it worsens, Hilton notices that Kingsley is becoming more and more nervous. They start singing and soon other men in nearby shell-holes begin to join in. Afterwards, as the bombardment continues, Kingsley begins his interview with Colonel Hilton, who reveals that he visited Abercrombie at the Chateau to discuss a letter which the Viscount had written, in which he had stated his intention of resigning his commission. However, before they have much of an opportunity to discuss this, a shell strikes and Kingsley is buried alive. It takes him a short while to dig himself free, whereupon he discovers that Hilton is dead. Kingsley manages to struggle back through the bombardment to the British trenches, but before heading back behind the lines, he reports the position of the 5th Battalion to the Royal Artillery and also reports the death of Colonel Hilton.

Critical Appraisal of Chapters 46-50

It must be said that for such a principled and upright man, Kingsley is extremely good at falling down. Considering how 'wretched' he felt following his first betrayal of Agnes, he takes very little persuading to betray her again, evidently for the sole reason that Kitty is so 'very pretty'. How is the reader supposed to believe in his principles and that his sacrifice of his family was so significant, when he behaves like this? It is equally difficult, however, to believe in Kitty. She has only known Kingsley for a few days; she is a man-eating Suffragette, who by her own admission, in all matters except sex, prefers the company of women, and yet we are supposed to believe that she has fallen madly in love with our hero, Kingsley. Presumably, the reason behind this is that Kingsley is meant to appear irresistible to women - hence the juvenile references to the size of his penis. Incidentally, only a male writer could possibly presume that size matters!

Again, the sex scenes are coy and, evidently unlike Kingsley's 'manhood', underdeveloped. If, however, we are to believe that Kingsley is prepared to repeatedly betray Agnes, we must understand why. Is Kitty better in bed than Agnes? Does Kingsley prefer Kitty's independent free spirit to Agnes's possibly more prim bedroom habits? There needs to be a comparison between the two women in Kingsley's mind. Equally, if Kitty is so much in love, then why? She's had twenty-four lovers: what is so special about Kingsley compared to the rest? We are given no details as to the physical or - more importantly - emotional connection between these two characters, so the situation makes no sense, other than as casual sex, which is fine, except that we are being told that the relationship is more significant than that.

The purpose of chapter forty-seven is, essentially, to establish Stamford's innocence, which would be quite reasonable, had this not been obvious for some considerable time. We also learn that Abercrombie had been writing less patriotic poetry prior to his death and are given some examples, which could easily suggest that Wilfred Owen should be sued for plagiarism given that he seems to have copied certain phrases from Abercrombie and used them in Dulce et Decorum Est, which was published in the autumn of 1917, several months after Abercrombie's death. Perhaps Owen was also a resident at Chateau Beaurivage (rather than Craiglockhart) and caught a sneaky peek at some of the Viscount's verses?

It does seems a little strange, in chapter forty-eight to discover that Nurse Murray rides a 'magnificent' motorbike. This would have been an unusual mode of transport for a lady in 1917 and to make it believable, Ben Elton would have done better to introduce the subject earlier in the novel - even if only in passing - rather than to thrust it upon us now, when it seems incongruous. One also has to question, given Kingsley's repeated admissions of his continued love for his wife, whether Kitty would really declare her undying love for him. I can only assume that the author's point here is that love is bigger than anything else: that Kitty is prepared to forego her principles for the sake of the man she loves. However if that utter nonsense really is the case, then we really need more evidence of their supposed love, other than three quick romps and a few favourable comments regarding the size of his 'manhood' and Kitty's prettiness - it is quite simply not enough.

Back in the thick of things again, it seems very peculiar to me that Kingsley is allowed to accompany Philby into No Man's Land without introducing himself or explaining the purpose of his mission. The journey across No Man's Land appears to be fraught with confusion and takes place in the dark, so it beggars belief that amidst the chaos, Kingsley and Philby manage to come across a runner sent by Colonel Philby - the very man they are seeking. It then seems equally odd that this runner cannot furnish Philby with the information that he requires as to the whereabouts of the 5th Battalion, thus allowing Philby to high-tail it back to the Artillery and save himself the trip. Given the situation that the runner describes, it is unthinkable that the colonel would risk a runner simply for water. He would be instructed to obtain reinforcements as well and, thus save the necessity of sending back a second man later on. The encounter with the German soldiers is also nonsense. Even if Philby doesn't think that it is his duty to 'take on the Prussian Guard', which is unlikely, the Germans would almost certainly recognise an artillery observer when they saw one and would not hesitate to take a shot. They could ill-afford for accurate information about their position to get back to the artillery and would have seen it as their duty to protect the rest of their men.

The whole point of this episode is to bring Kingsley and Colonel Hilton together. Philby could have got his information from the runner but must obviously carry on so that he can be wounded and so that Kingsley can save the day - yet again! This much is clear, even before Philby is shot, so transparent is the plot. There is, however, a rather boring trend within this novel, which rears its head here, yet again. This is the fact that, once again, Kingsley is left with no alternative other than to follow someone else out into No Man's Land. First it had been Edmonds, then McCroon and now Hilton. Why could Ben Elton not have found some other method of endangering his central character, because this one is becoming more than a little tedious after its third outing.

The time spent by Kingsley and Hilton in the shell-hole feels very contrived. For Kingsley to suddenly become nervous and twitchy seems odd, when he has been in equally dangerous positions before. However, it does allow the author to briefly re-introduce the concept of shell-shock. The idea of the men singing seems a little far-fetched, although not unheard-of in such situations. I, however, would have expected Kingsley to go straight into his interview in order to calm his nerves, because that would seem to be more in character. One has to wonder why the colonel wouldn't have mentioned Abercrombie's letter before. 'You didn't ask', seems a very weak excuse, given the circumstances surrounding the Viscount's death. However, it has allowed Ben Elton to drag out the motive behind the murder until the end of the story.

Finally, Kingsley has to be buried alive. Why? Because almost everything else has been done to him, so why not? However, he cannot be allowed to die, because then we'd never know who did it. So, he unburies himself with remarkable ease, dashes back to the artillery, reports the situation and saves the day - once again. The fact that Kingsley evidently didn't get a medal seems shameful. He ought to have been awarded one simply for always being in the right place at the right time!

CHAPTERS 51-52

Chapter 51

Captain Shannon has returned to France to establish what Kingsley has managed to find out. When Kingsley gets back to his billet, he arranges to meet Shannon at the Chateau later that evening. When they meet, Shannon is as arrogant as ever and they decide to take a walk in the grounds. Shannon is initially keen to discuss the thrill of battle and, although Kingsley will privately admit to feelings of exhilaration, he is in no mood to discuss this with Shannon and quickly turns the conversation to the Abercrombie case.

He reveals that the 'shadowy officer' was Stamford - Abercrombie's lover - which seems to come as a surprise to Shannon, although Kingsley tells him that Stamford did not kill the Viscount. Shannon tries, repeatedly, to bait Kingsley; to sway the conversation away from the case, but Kingsley doggedly perseveres, revealing that the second mystery officer - the one seen by Nurse Murray leaving Abercrombie's room - was Captain Shannon himself. Kingsley asserts that Shannon had already been at the chateau, investigating the communists Hopkins and McCroon - a fact that Shannon does not bother to deny. Kingsley believes that Abercrombie had been writing to a national newspaper and it was this letter that Colonel Hilton had intercepted. When it had been passed Staff Headquarters, they had naturally handed it on to Shannon. Shannon angrily denounces Abercrombie as a coward, before resuming his usual calm demeanour. Kingsley describes Shannon's movements on the night of the murder, as well as his attempt to frame Hopkins for the crime, which Kingsley asserts, was really the only thing that led to Shannon's undoing. By now, Shannon's hand is resting firmly on the butt of his gun, when all of a sudden, Nurse Murray appears, pointing a German pistol at Shannon. She tells him to withdraw his hand and, when he does not immediately do so, she shoots him in the groin. As he begins to scream, she shoots him again, in the head.

Kingsley is shocked and points out that, although there is justice in Nurse Murray's actions, Shannon should have been tried by a court,before being executed. It transpires that Kingsley had asked Nurse Murray to follow him and Captain Shannon on their walk, but with no idea that she had a personal score to settle with her rapist. Between them, they remove all forms of identification and then drive Shannon's body as close as they can get to the front lines, whereupon Kingsley carries him the rest of the way to a dressing station, where he is pronounced dead. When Kingsley and Nurse Murray are travelling back, he reveals that his name is Kingsley, not Marlowe, which causes her much confusion, as the only policeman named Kingsley that she has ever heard of, is dead.

Chapter 52

Kingsley drives Nurse Murray back to the chateau and they part amicably, before he leaves for England. He spends a week in London, during which time, he meets Sir Mansfield Cumming and explains Shannon's role (although he claims to have shot Shannon himself). He also writes to Agnes, revealing the whole story, except for his affair with Nurse Murray. He explains that he has concluded a strange bargain with Cumming, which is that Kingsley is prepared to cover up Shannon's role and the possible S.I.S. involvement in Abercrombie's death, provided that Abercrombie's last poems are published and that Kingsley be allowed to assume the identity of his dead brother, Robert. He hopes that Agnes will accept this idea, which she does, as she seems to assume that he is making some sort of proposal. When Kingsley returns home, as Robert, Agnes - although initially confused and angry - accepts both him and his proposal of marriage.

Critical Appraisal of Chapters 46-50

The idea of Abercrombie 'doing a Sassoon' and getting shot for his 'crime' is ridiculous. In Sassoon's case, contrary to popular and Ben Elton's evident opinion, he did not send his anti-war declaration to the newspapers. He sent it to his colonel and to several friends, among whom was a Labour politician, H. Lees-Smith, who read the Declaration in the House of Commons and it was subsequently reported in The Times. The authorities decided that the best course of action was to suggest that Sassoon was neurotic and send him to Craiglockhart Military Hospital, thereby, theoretically diminishing the impact of his protest. It does, therefore, seem very strange that, within weeks of Sassoon's protest, the authorities (officially or otherwise) would decide to shoot the next man to take a similar course of action. This is especially strange when one considers that in reality, the next man who actually did 'do a Sassoon' was court-martialled and dismissed from the army. This man - another poet, Max Plowman - made his protest, like Kingsley, on intellectual grounds, although he did state that he was against all war, rather than just British war aims. As such, it is easy to see that reality is very different from fiction, but perhaps not nearly as exciting.

The conversation between Shannon and Kingsley is quite ridiculous, with Shannon being the arrogant cad, while Kingsley resolutely retains his stiff upper lip. One can appreciate that all good detective stories must have a 'reveal' and usually the more drawn-out, the better. The problem here is that most readers will have already worked out that Shannon is the murderer quite some time beforehand, so the desired element of surprise, which the author is clearly trying to create, simply fails to materialise.

Shannon's death is so sudden that it really is inexplicable. This is the first we know of Nurse Murray's presence; or her possession of a German firearm; or the fact that she can obviously shoot very well; or the fact that Captain Shannon had actually raped her. Until now we have been led to believe that the sexual experience between Kitty and Shannon had been unpleasant, but there is an enormous leap between this and rape. This aspect would have been far more plausible if Kitty had either confided the rape to Kingsley or - perhaps better still - had said nothing at all about her relationship with Shannon, thereby leaving the reader guessing. The speed with which she decides to shoot Shannon is ludicrous, as one would have thought that she would want to see him suffer and squirm, given her personality, but also because it cheats the reader of any feeling of resolution. He is simply snatched away half-way through explaining his motives.

The ease with which Kingsley and Nurse Murray dump Shannon's body is equally wondrous. It is very strange how nothing is ever noticed in Ben Elton's version of the war, so no-one happens to spot Kingsley wandering in from the wrong direction, or that he is a military policeman who shouldn't be there in the first place. The convenience of it all is simply stupendous.

Finally, we come to the end of the story, and the last chapter, where everything is wrapped up with a speed and convenience that leaves one's head spinning. Why, I ask myself, having trawled through nearly 400 pages, are we only given five pages for the final explanation and for Kingsley to be reunited with his wife? The reader is left feeling cheated, as reasons are rushed or not explained properly at all, making this chapter really the ultimate insult to the reader's intelligence: because presumably the author could not be bothered to flesh out these final episodes properly.

The idea that the government and Abercrombie's family would agree to the publication of his anti-war poems is beyond belief. The whole point of the investigation - aside from the political angle - was to preserve Abercrombie's reputation and assuage his powerful father. Why would the politicians suddenly go back on this? They would sacrifice Cumming first: especially as they evidently have little time for the intelligence services anyway. Surely this would provide them with the perfect opportunity to disband the S.I.S. Why, in addition, would they consent to Kingsley returning to his wife, even in the guise of his dead brother? A lot of time and effort went into faking his death and they had invented a perfectly plausible plot for the time after the investigation - so why would he be allowed to change that? The whole 'Do as I say, or I'll expose a dead man' threat simply doesn't work. The authorities wouldn't care - they weren't that soft! Shannon and Cumming would have been expendable.

Kingsley's reunion with Agnes is at least consistent in that it is just as ludicrous as everything that has gone before. In the space of two pages, Agnes kisses him, slaps him, apologises then berates him, then reveals that she'd always known that Shannon was a 'wrong 'un', and then they go to bed! Surely the love of Kingsley's life deserves a bit more time and attention to detail than this? On what grounds are we supposed to believe in their relationship? Simply because we are told of its power and fortitude? This simply isn't enough.

CHARACTER ANALYSIS

Normally I provide a character analysis, based on my interpretation of the creation of the central characters within a novel. However, in this instance, the characters are so flimsy, stereotypical and poorly created that it is really rather difficult to write an ordinary character analysis in the manner in which I usually would. So, I have provided a basic description of the character as the author probably wished them to be understood, followed by a critical appraisal of the creation of the character, in the case of Douglas Kingsley, Captain Shannon and Nurse Murray.

DOUGLAS KINGSLEY

The character of Douglas Kingsley is introduced very early in the story and this introduction is not really very favourable. We are told that he is 'proud', 'arrogant' and conceited, that he always thinks he is in the right - which is made more unfortunate by the fact that he quite often is. Despite these obvious flaws, we also learn that he is 'loved' and that his arguments, although often unpopular, are usually not unreasonable.

At his trial, Kingsley comes across as pompous and 'superior': attitudes which serve him poorly in the circumstances. He is an inspector in the Metropolitan police force, having served for fourteen years, and is married to Agnes Beaumont, the daughter of the Police Commissioner, with whom he has one son, named George. The couple live a seemingly idyllic life in Hampstead Heath, where they keep a couple of servants. Kingsley is renowned for his dedication to duty and attention to detail, having earned a reputation as 'the Yard's best man'.

Kingsley's stance against the war is one of intellect and intelligence, rather than morals or religion and as the story develops, one would have to say that, really, this aspect of Kingsley's character changes little. Despite his imprisonment, the cost to his family and the dangers to himself, he sticks resolutely to his opinions regarding the war. Notwithstanding the restrictions of prison life, this part of the story also enables the author to show us some other aspects of Kingsley's personality, such as his sense of fairness and honour, in that he refuses to name the Irish informants, even though this would guarantee his own safety, because to do so would ensure their certain deaths.

When he is freed from prison, Kingsley still harbours doubts about the ethics of the role he has been given, struggling to justify the need to search out one murderer amid the slaughter. The new-found freedom which accompanies Kingsley's liberation also enables us to see yet more of his personality, in that he seems to instinctively do the 'right thing'. Again, as he did in the prison, he behaves with honour, protecting Violet from Shannon's malevolence. Kingsley's behaviour in the war scenes continues along the same lines, as he always manages to save the day. He performs heroically during the raid, despite the fact that to participate is contrary to everything he believes in. Later, he is able to report the position of the 5th Battalion to the Royal Artillery and, hopefully, prevent them falling victim to their own shells.

Finally, of course, Kingsley wins through and cracks the case, solving the mystery of who shot Captain Abercrombie. In so doing, he is able to round off the story nicely and honourably by arranging for the posthumous publication of Abercrombie's poems and keeping his promise to George by returning home.

Critical Appraisal of the Creation of the Character of Douglas Kingsley

The initial portrait of Kingsley as an unfavourably arrogant, pompous, self-opinionated plod, is created with one purpose in mind: so that the author can spend the rest of the novel disproving this conception and converting the reader to the belief that the hero is actually a thoroughly decent, albeit naturally flawed, chap. This would be fine, except for one minor problem: the initial representation of Kingsley is so transparently thin, that not only do we not really believe in it, we also don't really care - and that is the most fatal flaw of all in a work of fiction.

It is really hard to believe, based on the information we are given, that this upstanding police inspector would behave in the way he does. His reasons for refusing to fight are flimsy and insufficiently argued, so the reader cannot really understand why he is prepared to sacrifice his wife, son, career and freedom on such a basis. Even when his beautiful Agnes appears, he remains mysteriously wedded to these ideals about which the reader is still told almost nothing, other than that he believes in them.

We are then shown various other aspects of Kingsley's personality, presumably as part of the author's effort to redeem the character. So, he appears honourable, brave, resolute, caring, professional, etc. However, considering that he is supposedly such an intellectual man, he is also remarkably stupid, as he doubts the reasons why he has been freed from prison, before dashing about all over France and Flanders, endangering his investigation, his life and lives of almost everyone with whom he comes into contact.

Kingsley's 'fling' with Nurse Murray takes us into the realms of the surreal. This is a man who, evidently, loves his wife very deeply: he had always known she was 'the right girl for him' and had set about pursuing this celebrated beauty with 'every fibre in his being'. Having caught her and married her in 1912, their son had been born within a year, but even now, four years later, he longs to 'cover her sweet face with burning kisses' and is 'scarcely able to bear' the parting from her. Agnes is not a hag, an ugly crone, or a wretched vile creature, but a beautiful young woman with 'soft golden curls', whose personality betrays a coquettish 'lack of seriousness' in times when her husband had not been behaving like a peevish martyr to his conscience. So, having filled our heads with these images of a 'perfect', fun, happy marriage and an upstanding, honourable gentleman, who utters priceless phrases, such as 'Unhand that girl', Ben Elton then expects us to believe that Kingsley is prepared to brush all of this to one side and have sex with a relative stranger, simply because she offers? Admittedly, one could argue that Kingsley has given up on Agnes. But has he? He was filled with joy at the prospect that Agnes missed him: he promised George that he would return home - and Kingsley is, as we know, a man of his word. So that argument doesn't really stand up to much scrutiny, especially considering Kingsley's 'miserable' post-coital guilt. So, this honourable, guilt-riden man might be expected, therefore to put this one-off fling down to experience and control himself in future? Well... no. What he actually does is leap into bed with Kitty at the very next opportunity - which is, of course, completely out of character, but what the heck! The reason for his downfall, other than Kitty's obvious willingness to participate, is evidently that she is so 'very, very pretty', which seems a little weak, given what he potentially has to lose.

There are two other sides to Kingsley's character shown by this affair, which do not fit and seem out of place. The first is that of weakness. He does not appear to be a man who would be prone to having a vulnerability, but it would seem that the author would like us to believe that he will happily have sex three times with the first female who offers him the opportunity - even though he 'had definitely not been intending to make love to her again'. Or is it perhaps that Ben Elton is saying that all men, given the opportunity, will jump into bed with a woman who offers herself, regardless of the consequences? That, I'm afraid, says very little for Mr Elton's opinion of his own sex and is blatantly untrue and unfair. The second problem is that both we and Kingsley know that Shannon and Nurse Murray have shared a bed at some point in the fairly recent past and I can easily imagine Kingsley being the type of man who would reject Kitty on that basis alone, such is his abhorrence of Captain Shannon.

The investigation and solving of the crime is, presumably, supposed to show us what an absolutely brilliant detective Kingsley really is, but once again things do seem to go too well to be believable. All the pieces of evidence drop into place rather too neatly and, before we know it, the solution is at hand. In the 'reveal' conversation with Shannon, Kingsley's character is meant to be the professional policeman, doing his job, regardless of the provocation. The problem with this is that he actually really comes across as insufferably annoying - besides which most readers will have already worked out who the murderer is long ago anyway!

The creation of Kingsley's character is flimsy from start to finish. His background is non-existent and the few details which are given as to his personality, are either contradicted or else completely disproved, as the story unfolds. Much of what we are told is simply declared as fact, rather than established through the evidence of either the narrative or the way in which the character behaves. The result of this is that, unfortunately, not only does Kingsley feel as much of a stranger at the end of the novel as he did at the beginning, but I, for one, could not have cared less whether he lived, or died, or went to reside in Timbuktu.

CAPTAIN SHANNON

Our first official meeting with Captain Shannon occurs when he goes to inform Agnes Kingsley of her husband's death, although he had actually been responsible for shooting Kingsley as well. We are told that Shannon is 'strikingly handsome' and has a 'genuinely sympathetic manner', but we can also see that he is self deprecating and is excellent in the way he behaves with George. However all of this must clearly be an act, as by the very next chapter, we are beginning to see Shannon in his true colours. Now, we can see arrogance and hautiness, which all too soon, as he and Kingsley watch the Pierrot show at Folkestone, becomes even worse, deteriorating into crude offensiveness.

Over brunch, Shannon explains his philosophy to Kingsley, which seems to revolve mainly around pleasuring himself at the expense of others. This selfish arrogance culminates in the near-rape of Violet, a waitress from the hotel, whose reputation and innocence is only saved by the timely intervention of Inspector Kingsley.

Despite his many, many flaws, it would seem that Captain Shannon is rather good at his job. He effects excellent pursuits of Kingsley through the streets of London, without the policeman being even vaguely aware of his presence. However, at all times, he only does what is absolutely necessary, leaving Kingsley to his own devices where possible, so that he may seek out his own particular pleasures.

Later in the story, Shannon returns to France, ostensibly on behalf of Sir Mansfield Cumming, but really because, as the killer, he wants to know if he has been discovered. Right to the end, he remains arrogant, trying to bluff his way out of the situation, all the while on his guard, threatening Kingsley. At the last, we discover his guilt in the rape of Nurse Murray, who exacts her revenge in a manner which she deems most appropriate.

Critical Appraisal of the Creation of the Character of Captain Shannon

Once again, as with all of the characters in The First Casualty, we have been treated to a very thin and flimsy character construction. The initial creation of the pretence of a kindly and caring gentleman needs to be built upon further, before being destroyed and it would actually be better if we could have seen Agnes Kingsley being more beguiled by Shannon's charms. Shannon is going to be our murderer, but we are supposed to remain blissfully unaware of this until much nearer the end of the story, so, to me, it would make more sense that he should continue to appear as the considerate gentleman for as long as possible. The problem in this novel is that Shannon's 'mad and bad' side is revealed too early and, therefore, the reader immediately begins to suspect that all is not as it seems. If we could see Agnes Kingsley at least beginning to fall for his charms, we would trust Shannon more; we might also accept her husband's fall from grace a little more easily, thereby creating much more romantic tension and a far better 'whodunit' atmosphere.

We obviously appreciate that with someone like Agnes, unlike Violet, for example, Shannon would have to really use all of his appeal and charisma to win her over, but this would make his character so much more believable than this man for whom girls just seem to fall on their backs, simply because he smiles vaguely in their direction. We are supposed to believe that Shannon is a scoundrel par excellence, but what we are really shown is a bunch of weak women, tales of whom he is ready to recount, who simply don't know how to say 'no'. One wonders if Ben Elton has been watching too much James Bond ('Oh... James...')!

Then, of course, we come to the hapless Violet, who falls for Shannon's 'striking' good looks just like all the others, but then is surprised when he expects more. The fact that Violet is a waitress in Folkestone - a town from which many many soldiers embarked for France during the war - and yet remains so wide-eyed and innocent in such matters seems ridiculous. I'm not for one minute suggesting that she should consent to Shannon's demands, I am, however, questioning the fact that she could be so naive as to live and work where she does, mix with as many soldiers as she would in her line of work and not have any idea as to why one of them might ask her to a lonely spot on the beach?

In the matter of Shannon's behaviour during the rape scene itself, I would think that most self-respecting women would be tempted to ask him to shut up, with all his ranting. We later learn that Shannon had previously raped Nurse Murray but it seems very hard to believe that someone as feisty as her would have fallen for the same lines and smiles as the young, innocent Violet, especially if accompanied by the same never-ending rigmarole. There is something rather too melodramatic in many of the characteristics and mannerisms of Captain Shannon, to the point where one has to wonder whether we are supposed to take him seriously. There is also something rather fanciful - or at least optimistic on the part of the author - whose character claims to be able to have sex quite so frequently as Shannon does.

When it comes to the question of the murder itself, there is really very little to be said. I simply cannot understand why Shannon would have killed Abercrombie. A hero turning against the 'cause' seems a ludicrous pretence at a motive and personally I would have found it much more believable - given the rest of the plot - if Shannon had been a raving psychopathic, serial killer, hell-bent on murdering every homosexual in the British Army. It certainly would not have been any less plausible than the far-fetched, half-baked motive we are offered here.

NURSE KITTY MURRAY

We first meet Nurse Murray when Kingsley arrives at the Chateau Beaurivage to investigate Abercrombie's death. She appears to be a no-nonsense forthright young woman with a deep-seated resentment of all policemen. This, we later discover, is due to the fact that, as a Suffragette, she has been maltreated by members of the police force on several occasions. There are some definite masculine overtones to Nurse Murray: she has forsaken her more feminine christian name of Kathleen in favour of the less attractive Kitty; she wears her hair short and has a boyish figure; she rides a motorcycle and has quite a masculine and modern attitude towards sex.

She is, however, quite sensible too and is unprepared to risk pregnancy, despite her penchant for sexual intercourse. Her attitude to adultery is also very avant garde for the period and her class, in that she seems to think it perfectly acceptable, provided nobody finds out. Those in the upper classes were renowned for their affairs, but Kitty seems to me to be more upper-middle class and one wonders whether her attitudes to female and sexual liberation are perhaps a means to escaping a life that might otherwise have been stiflingly dull.

As the story progresses, Kitty falls in love with Kingsley, despite her better judgement. She had intended this to be just another of her many flings, but soon finds that her feelings amount to more than that. However, when he makes it clear than nothing can come of their relationship, she disguises her embarrassment with a mixture of bluff and bravado, neither of which work, as Kingsley is only too aware that he has hurt her feelings by his rejection.

Nurse Murray plays a pivotal role in the conclusion of the murder mystery, as she shoots and kills Captain Shannon. Her motives in doing so are revenge and justice, in that not only had he murdered Viscount Abercrombie, but he had also raped her, so in Nurse Murray's eyes at least, she has simply saved the hangman a job.

Critical Appraisal of the Creation of the Character of Nurse Kitty Murray

Nurse Murray is not just a nondescript love-interest with whom our hero has a few quick romps during the course of his investigation. She actually provides several vital pieces of information, such as the fact that Shannon was at the chateau before Abercrombie was killed, and the link between the poetry, which Stamford was claiming as his own, being so different to everything he had written before. She also winds up shooting the dastardly and deserving Shannon, thereby rounding off the whole story. Therefore, one is bound to ask why we know so little about this young woman. Admittedly, this makes her character consistent with all the others, but one would have been interested to know something more of her background.

All we know is that she is a Suffragette who, before the war, was imprisoned seven times under the Cat and Mouse Act of 1913 and that she likes sex - quite a lot! I have made the assumption that she is probably more upper/middle class than upper class, simply because she seems too worldly wise to be a 'toff' and I think Ben Elton would have portrayed her less favourably had this been the case. Also, although this is bit of a generalisation, most upper class girls did not get promoted to the rank of Staff Nurse, but tended to remain as VADs, often cruelly neglected and accused of 'playing' at nursing, rather being of any real use. This does not seem to be so in Nurse Murray's case. Nonetheless, I'm really guessing here and it would be nice to have this background clarified and fleshed-out properly, even if only so that we could understand her personality a little better. It is a matter of pure convenience that Nurse Murray should happen to be a Suffragette and the reasons behind this are two-fold. Firstly, it allows the author to include another historical aspect into his storyline. Secondly, it gives him the opportunity to have a good old rant about the treatment of women at the hands of the authorities. The problem with the first point is that this book is already bursting at the seams with superfluous historical facts, figures and name-dropping. The second issue creates another problem in that unfortunately, Ben Elton has chosen to portray his feminist central character as an extremely gung-ho, 'jolly-hockey-sticks' public school girl type who is, frankly insufferably stupid and goes all dewey eyed simply because her lover seems have have a rather over-developed penis, which matches his rather under-developed brain. Had women not already won the vote by the time Mr Elton penned his novel, he could quite easily have set their campaign back fifty years!

Nurse Murray's attitude to sex might seem a bit too modern to some readers, but actually this was not unusual amongst women who found themselves freed from the shackles and constraints of home life for the first time. For many it was an opportunity to experience life without parents and chaperones and many went wild! I can easily imagine, however, that most men would find an exclamation of 'Tally ho!' during their ardent lovemaking to be most off-putting, and one would have thought that after twenty-four attempts, at least one kind soul might have advised her to refrain from this juvenile behaviour.

I do find it almost inconceivable that Captain Shannon could have raped Nurse Murray. Not only is this because the subject is introduced so randomly, but also because his method of seduction appears to be to talk his victims into submission, and I simply cannot imagine this strong-willed independent young women allowing him to get away with anything so obvious - or to get a word in, for that matter!

THEMES

MURDER AND JUSTICE

On the dustjacket to the hardback version of Ben Elton's novel *The First Casualty*, there is a brief outline of the story, which includes the following statements: 'What is murder? What is justice in the face of unimaginable daily slaughter? And where is the honour in saving a man from the gallows if he is only to be returned to die in a suicidal battle?' There are then some further comments on the blurring of the 'gap between legally sanctioned and illegal murder'. As such, the reader is being given an enormous clue that, in theory at least, these are going to be some of the major themes of this novel.

Ben Elton is a politically-aware author, who shows no reserve in telling us his opinion in various ways throughout the novel. Here, he wants the reader to question their traditional perspective of murder. Which killing is 'legally sanctioned'? That of Viscount Abercrombie, or those of the men dying on the battlefields of Northern France? Is it more or less 'right' to kill someone for the reasons stated by Captain Shannon, than it is to kill an enemy soldier in war? Within the context of this novel, the 'illegal' murder is supposedly that of Captain Abercrombie, killed evidently because he desired to resign his commission in protest against the war. What Ben Elton wants us to move onto, in our thought process, is that, if this is the case, then the men being killed on the battlefields, must be as the result of 'legally sanctioned' murders. Or is it, perhaps, the other way around? Are we supposed to believe that Abercrombie's death was 'legally sanctioned' by the S.I.S.? In which case, are the 'murders' taking place on the battlefields illegal, maybe because, according to Kingsley at least, the terms under which Britain went to war, were bogus?

Ben Elton is a writer of polemic perspectives, evidently implying that if one type of murder is illegal, then the other must be legal - or at least 'legally sanctioned'. There would seem to be no half-way house. There is no straightforward killing because we are at war - every death has to be a 'murder' - or at best a 'suicide'.

It is really for each individual reader to decide (if they wish), which of the killings is 'legal' murder and which is 'illegal'. In either case, however, the use of the word 'murder' in this context is extremely emotive, since by definition it involves the unlawful, premeditated taking of another life. We have to, therefore, assume that Ben Elton believes that the Army Chiefs of Staff, from Douglas Haig downwards, were as guilty of murder as someone who planned the stabbing, strangulation, shooting or stabbing of their unsuspecting victim in a dark alleyway or quiet country backwater.

There are doubtless many who would agree with this viewpoint, especially insofar as it relates to Douglas Haig, who among populist myths, is sometimes thought of as something of a 'butcher', by which we may infer 'murderer'. We may assume that Ben Elton agrees with these myths - he went on to perpetuate them in Blackadder Goes Forth. As to the accuracy of such portrayals, a great deal of opinion has changed in recent years and many historians now believe that Haig was greatly maligned in the years after the war - especially by David Lloyd George - continuing well into the 1960s and beyond. This is a matter of great debate and would take up more space than I have available here. For now I will say that the setting of this novel is meant to be a war, not a tea-party and that one of the hardest parts about being in charge in times of war is making those tough decisions: planning a battle, knowing that men will die, but going ahead with it anyway. These were not decision which were taken lightly.

There are many - perhaps including Ben Elton - who would, I am sure, argue that the senior officers made their decisions to 'murder' their men from the relative comfort of a headquarters based miles behind the front lines - hence his unfavourable portrayal of officers, gorging themselves, when compared to the men, who have insufficient water to drink, while facing the enemy machine guns, sniper fire and massive bombardments. It should be borne in mind, however, that a general needs to see the 'whole' battle, not just a few yards of it. This might seem unfair to the 'poor bloody infantryman' who is stuck at the pointy end, but the hard fact is that someone has to take charge and, it is pointless becoming all emotional about it and saying how 'unfair' it all is. It's a war. It's not meant to be fair.

The other problem which I have with this representation of murder is that the actual murder in the story doesn't really work. Everything is telegraphed almost from the beginning of the novel - which is rather pointless in a murder mystery: the motive is bizarre; the method is ludicrous. Why kill a man and leave him in a hospital, when you could drive him to a battlefield and leave the body where it would never be found? Why make the murderer so obvious that the reader has worked it out long before the end of the novel? Having belittled one type of murder so much, the reader cannot seriously be expected to consider the concept of any 'murder' on the battlefields as a proper concept for consideration. Besides which, the arguments are, as stated, so polemic and emotive, that no-one can be expected to consider them as worthy of serious discussion.

Then we come to the subject of justice. In this aspect we are, in the context of this novel, supposed to look at two factors: 'the honour of saving a man from the gallows if he is only to be returned to die in a suicidal battle', and the sanity or otherwise, of investigating one particular murder among so many. Where is the 'justice' for those who die 'in the face of unimaginable slaughter'. Again, we are dealing here with some extremely emotive language, giving rise to strong opinions.

Ordinarily, Inspector Kingsley of the Metropolitan Police would feel justifiably proud if he managed to prove a man innocent and save him from a wrongful hanging. This is especially so when one considers Kingsley's statement in court that the 'men and... women who were condemned to death as a result of my investigations were all heartily deserving of their fate', which suggests his belief not only that he had been right in his assumptions about their guilt, but also that the death penalty in itself, was reasonable and just. Therefore, to prove Hopkins innocent would presumably have the same effect as if Kingsley had been working on the streets of London. His dogged investigations, undertaken at no small risk to his own personal safety, had shown that this man could not have fired the fatal shot. Given Kingsley's low opinion of the war, we can only imagine his feelings upon discovering that Hopkins had almost immediately been returned to the front. Then to actually witness him being blown to smithereens by a bomb blast would, of course, be the ultimate irony. As such, one could argue, that Ben Elton has put his case well, as there was no point in releasing Hopkins, just for him to die anyway - or was there? And has he?

If Hopkins had been executed as a murderer, it wouldn't really have made much difference - he would still be dead. However, his body and records would have been treated differently to those men who were killed in action. If his family had requested details of his death, the authorities would have informed them that he had been executed, rather than killed in action. But he was innocent and, regardless of the fact that he went on to die, he deserved to die as a free man, not to be placed up against a wall and be shot for a crime he did not commit.

Did Ben Elton actually do a very good job of putting the case for justice in the case of Hopkins, however? Well, unfortunately the point is, once again, lost as the representation of Hopkins's death is not even remotely realistic and cannot be taken seriously. McCroon would almost certainly have been at least wounded by the blast and the timing of the situation is almost laughable. The sole purpose of this death is therefore, rather too obviously, to prove Ben Elton's point: that they might as well have shot Hopkins in the first place, for what it was worth. Again, the presentation and portrayal of this scene, being so emotive, polemic and obvious belittles the whole scene and this theme, which could have been much better served by Kingsley perhaps hearing of Hopkins's death a little later on, rather than this over-dramatic rendition.

As to the value, or even necessity, of investigating one 'murder' amongst so many 'murders', the investigation of such crimes at the front was carried out by the Military Police as part of their duties, when necessary - without the assistance of Scotland Yard. The availability of firearms and ammunition usually coupled with excesses of alcohol led to several soldiers being court-martialled and executed for murder during the conflict. According to the book Blindfold and Alone by Cathryn Corns and John Hughes-Wilson, thirty-seven Allied soldiers were executed during the First World War for the crime of murder. In most cases, these executions followed investigations by military police or occasionally by senior officers. In some cases the crime was witnessed by so many people that it really warranted no official investigation. The penalty in civilian courts for murder was hanging. Death by firing squad was simply the military equivalent.

The fact is that, in the case of this novel, although we are told that it 'explores some fundamental questions' such as those mentioned above, it doesn't really. Or if it does, it does so in such a contrived, misinformed and emotive fashion that, unfortunately, any hope at a reasoned argument is lost.

THE QUESTION OF TRUTH

The title of this novel is derived from the quotation: 'The first casualty when war comes is truth', which is attributed to US Senator Hiram Warren Johnson, who is alleged to have said this phrase in 1918. He was an Isolationist, who opposed America's entry into the First World War and, later US involvement in the Second World War and her entry into the United Nations.

Within the context of this novel, the author is referring us to several aspects of the truth in war. The first, and perhaps most important of these to be addressed, is the question of Britain's war aims, about which both Kingsley and Abercrombie seem to harbour doubts. Kingsley raises his dilemma at his trial, when he challenges the conventional reasons behind Britain's entry into the war - namely in defence of Belgium under the Treaty of London 1839. Under Article Seven of this Treaty, the neutrality of the newly created country of Belgium was guaranteed and thus, when Germany invaded her borders, Britain felt obliged to defend her. Or that, at least, is one version of history. Others might argue that the treaty merely provided Britain with a useful excuse to enter the war; to teach Germany a lesson, because actually Britain didn't really care less about Belgian neutrality and was far more concerned with the increasing size of the German fleet and the possibility of German ships being able to sail from nearby Belgian ports.

As the war progressed, and certainly by 1917, when this novel is set, quite a few people, including the oft-mentioned Siegfried Sassoon, were beginning to wonder about the veracity of Britain's stated war aims. In his declaration, written during the summer of 1917, Sassoon wrote: 'I believe that this War, upon which I entered as a war of defence and liberation, has now become a war of aggression and conquest.'

We can see this mirrored in The First Casualty as Kingsley questions these supposed 'truths' of Britain's averred war aims and the judge, and members of the outraged public, defend them against the 'traitor' in the dock. Opinion was as divided then as it is now on the causes of the war, making one man's truth, another man's fiction.

This is demonstrated in Chapter thirty-six, when the men take their 'communal interlude' during which they discuss exactly what they are fighting for. The learned corporal explains to all the others that it was the treaty system between the major European powers that really led to the war and that Britain's involvement was necessitated in order to protect Belgium. Kingsley disputes this latter statement and the resident socialist mocks them all as fools and puppets.

Abercrombie, we learn, having fought in the war, now believes it to be a 'pointless sacrifice'. His argument, we are led to believe, is similar to the one which had been made by Sassoon - namely that the war was being 'deliberately prolonged' for political purposes. However, where the two arguments differ, is that Sassoon's version of the truth behind the conflict was that the fighting men were being deceived and sacrificed, while Abercrombie evidently feels that his comrades are 'sheep, cattle' and 'fools'. So, even these two fairly similar versions of a truth can actually be seen to have quite stark and contrasting differences.

Another way in which Ben Elton examines the truth in the context of his novel is in Kingsley's deception of his wife. Nurse Murray makes the point to Kingsley that 'the war means different rules'. She exacts a promise that he won't tell his wife about their adulterous affair because Agnes 'wouldn't understand anyway'. This is because she feels that a different kind of truth applies to people who have experienced the war. They, she says, have to take their 'comfort' where they can. Kingsley's repeated sensations of guilt suggest that he finds it impossible to reconcile this suggestion to his ideas of a happy and trusting marriage, which is what he had believed in. His only form of consolation is that Agnes had abandoned him long before he committed adultery, but even this he knows to be a falsehood. As such, Kingsley is really lying to himself in this context, presumably to justify his own actions. The honour and truth of his marriage have been lost, and he knows that he can never reveal the whole story to Agnes because she would not tolerate such a deception and, therefore, the lie must be perpetuated.

The murder mystery aspect of the novel also provides us with another way of looking at this theme. Kingsley undertakes to discover the truth in the case of Abercrombie's murder and, in doing so, he frees Hopkins from the shame of a false execution. However, when the time comes to reveal the truth, Kingsley is prepared to camouflage it, mainly for reasons of personal gain. The truth - or at least the pursuit of the truth - has become less important to him. I suppose one could argue that one of his bargains is that Abercrombie's final poems must be published, which demonstrate the poets' true feelings about the war. However, I wonder whether the old Kingsley who hadn't seen the horrors of war, would have been prepared to commit to a deal such as this.

Finally, because it is not really connected to the First World War (although I believe it is connected to this novel), I come to another form of truth. That is the truth behind modern wars - such as the war in Iraq. I believe that the author, who is not renowned for his political reticence, is making a point here, that wars are often fought for the wrong reasons; often countries and men are taken into wars for stated objectives, which are false or ambiguous. That is his argument as regards the First World War, but he puts his point so forcibly and so out of context with the story itself, that one cannot help but wonder if he is trying to draw parallels between this and the more recent conflict mentioned above.

As I write this, the Chilcot Enquiry into the Iraq war is well underway and I am struck, more than ever, by thoughts of truth, beliefs - and the convenience or inconvenience of both. Listening to the evidence being given and also re-reading history books about the First World War, one can see that there have always been people who believe everything that they are told, just because someone in authority tells them; while others will always doubt, or prefer to make up their own minds - even if some believe them to be anarchic for doing so. However, neither side can always be right. This is because sometimes, what you are being told isn't the truth - it's a convenient (sometimes necessary) lie; and sometimes it's because you lie to yourself to justify something you desperately want to believe in.

So, now - as then - the only real truths about war are that people will always be damaged - both physically and mentally - that good men and women will always die, and that really, no-one ever wins because the cost is always too great. It's not really about victory: just about degrees of loss.

COMPARISONS

Within the realms of A-level studies, it is often required of students that they compare and contrast one piece of literature with another, which naturally requires a far greater level of understanding of both pieces and can also necessitate wider reading. Making such comparisons is good practice for students, forcing them into the habit of reading as widely as possible, from as many different sources as are available. This helps with the interpretation and understanding of literature, as well as enabling the student to have a broader perspective of the time during which a piece was written, and how this can influence the writing.

THE PORTRAYAL OF CONSCIENTIOUS OBJECTORS

The First Casualty is a novel which features the concept of conscientious objection as one of its pivotal plot lines - for a very good reason. It is essential to the story that Douglas Kingsley should be placed in prison and the author's best means of achieving this - considering that his hero is a policeman - is to have him incarcerated on the grounds of objection against the war. However, herein lie a few problems, since Kingsley cannot raise his objection on the grounds of 'conscience', having already sent several men (and women) to the gallows in the course of his duty. The author has, therefore, created a challenge to the war on the basis of intellect and logic, his character arguing that the war is offensive to him, because it is 'stupid'. The judge, however, quite rightly points out that the only acceptable grounds which a man may use under the 'conscience clause' of the Military Service Act 1916, are those of a moral or religious nature and Kingsley's reasons clearly fit into neither of these categories. The next problem lies in the very fact of Kingsley's having been conscripted in the first place. I find it highly unlikely that a senior Metropolitan policeman, such as Kingsley, would have been called up, which makes this whole trial scene unnecessary.

The trial itself is not strictly accurate, since the usual form would be that a man registering his conscientious objection to participating in the war, would be seen by a tribunal. This would be made up of a board of local dignitaries and one army representative. Each conscientious objector could fall into any one of three categories:

- **non-combatants**, who were prepared to be called up into the army, but not for the purpose of military duties, such as cooks, stretcher bearers, etc.

- **'alternativists'**, who were prepared to undertake civilian work, which was not under military control, such as working on farms or in non-military factories.

- **'absolutists'**, the most extreme conscientious objectors, who were opposed to the war and conscription and were not prepared to undertake any type of work which might be deemed to support the war.

The tribunal, therefore, had three choices:

- a non-combatant could be put on the military register and admitted to the non-combatant corps.

- alternativists could be exempted from military service, provided that they undertook to perform designated civilian work.

- absolutists could be granted unconditional exemption.

This latter decision was extremely rare and sometimes absolutists found themselves enlisted in the non-combatant corps. The usual course of action would be that they would then refuse to perform any duties or even to wear their uniform, they would then be court-martialled and imprisoned.

As such, Kingsley's position and trial doesn't really fit into any of these categories. We are supposed to believe that the authorities have set up a special trial for him, because he is a public figure, presumably to make an example of him. This doesn't make sense, however, as I think the authorities would be more likely to want to hush-up Kingsley's situation than to give it unnecessary publicity. Also if this argument is to be believed, then why is he only given a two year prison sentence and not the ten years that was meted out to one group of absolutists who disobeyed military orders in 1916? And are we supposed to believe that Kingsley would have refused alternative work on a farm or as a stretcher-bearer and would have chosen to be an absolutist, when his argument seems so spurious and when he so easily drops it upon reaching the trenches anyway?

This portrayal of conscientious objectors, while necessary to the plot, is unfortunately, so rushed and inaccurately represented that one feels this storyline has simply been employed as a means to an end. In addition, it provides the author with an opportunity to mention another aspect of the war - a habit which he repeats throughout the novel with monotonous regularity in an attempt to include as much detail about the conflict as possible.

Other novels include this theme, although more likely under the guise of general pacifism, which we will come to later. However, in *The Eye in the Door*, conscientious objectors do feature and here, Pat Barker has done a good job of showing the reader the extent to which some men were really prepared to go, for the sake of their beliefs. In this novel, the character of William Roper is a conscientious objector, who is placed in prison by the authorities. At his tribunal, William had made his objection to the war on moral, rather than religious grounds, but the board had refused his plea for absolute exemption and had sent him to the non-combatant corps, whereupon he had refused their first order to put on an army uniform and had been locked up in a freezing cell in the middle of January, with no clothes whatsoever. This treatment might sound unrealistically harsh, as though the author has embellished the reality for the purpose of enhancing her story. However, in his book, *We Will Not Fight... The Untold Story of World War One's Conscientious Objectors*, Will Ellsworth-Jones tells of many men who underwent similar privations. Bread and water diets and solitary confinement were well-known punishments for conscientious objectors, who were often kept in enforced states of silence in prison, mainly so that they would not be able to discuss their rebellious opinions between themselves, although to the conscientious objectors, it was not their opinions that they missed talking about - it was the general warmth of human conversation. Therefore, Pat Barker's representation of this man left cowering in a dark, freezing cold cell is not only historically accurate, but is also shows us the lengths to which a character might be prepared to take his beliefs, assuming that the reader is supposed to take him seriously.

Both authors also provide portrayals of pacifism - again with varying degrees of accuracy and success. In *The First Casualty*, it is not really Kingsley who is the pacifist, but Abercrombie. He has witnessed the horrors of war and has decided that he can participate no longer. Obvious comparisons are made in the novel with the situation and actions of Siegfried Sassoon. According to this novel, Abercrombie had tried, unsuccessfully, to write a letter to a newspaper, declaring his intention of resigning his commission. This letter had eventually found its way into the hands of Captain Shannon, who had decided - with or without official sanction - to kill Abercrombie, rather than permit him to denounce the cause of the war. This offers the reader only a brief, disjointed glimpse at the pacifist movement - and not a very positive one at that. Sassoon's character is raised frequently in either direct or oblique references, which are, again, unfavourable. However, when adverse references are made by such shallow characters as Captain Shannon, the author is clearly indicating that he actually wishes the reader to believe the opposite. In which case we are, presumably, meant to sympathise with Abercrombie - even if only because Captain Shannon, who is his main detractor, is clearly quite insane! Unfortunately, this obvious portrayal actually tells us nothing about pacifism during the First World War and, by the end of the story, we have absolutely no idea why Abercrombie had turned against the conflict.

In *The Regeneration Trilogy*, Pat Barker shows us two different kinds of pacifist. Firstly in *Regeneration*, we see Siegfried Sassoon arriving at Craiglockhart Military Hospital, having made his Declaration against the continuation of the war. Through his conversations with Dr Rivers, we learn of his inner conflicts and anger about the treatment of the men who are serving. Sassoon's eventual decision to return to the war has a great impact on both men, which can be further seen in the second part of the trilogy, *The Eye in the Door*, in which the author introduces other pacifist characters to the story. Here, almost everyone from Billy Prior's past has adopted a more pacifist attitude than he has, which leads Pat Barker's central character into greater feelings of isolation. Billy actually becomes angry towards many of these pacifists, especially when they seem to expect his sympathy towards their plight. Through these representations of pacifism, we can see the frequently-held feelings of confusion about those who adopted this line. Pat Barker seems far more sympathetic in her depiction of a pacifist who has seen service, such as Sassoon, than she does in her representation of the civilian conscientious objectors and pacifists, many of whom are characterised as self-serving trouble makers.

But what of the reality? Reading Sassoon's own version of the events that led to the writing of his declaration provides a different perspective, which is perhaps the most valuable of all in analysing this theme. In his autobiographical *Memoirs of an Infantry Officer*, Sassoon, as George Sherston, feels that he is 'the mouthpiece for the troops in the trenches', but it is also clear that he is greatly influenced by others, such as Henry Massingham (Markington) and Bertrand Russell (Tyrell). There seems some definite 'mission' and purpose in his protest within this memoir, which was written in 1930, some thirteen years after the events which Sassoon is describing. In his diaries, written at the time, however, there is an atmosphere of greater immediacy and one can more easily see the deterioration of his spirit, especially when he is in England, living with the knowledge that 'Men were attacking while I lay in bed and listened to the heavenly choruses of birds. Men were blundering about in a looming twilight of hell lit by livid flashes of guns and hideous with the malignant invective of machine-gun fire... And tonight the rain is hushing the darkness, steady, whispering rain - the voice of peace among the summer foliage.' It seems, when reading passages such as this, that it was, at least in part, the contrast between the hell and noise of war and the peace and complacency of home, that really drove Sassoon to action. Within a month of writing the above, he had composed his Declaration.

LANGUAGE AND WRITING STYLE

Ben Elton's writing style is quite unusual for a novel in the genre of First World War literature, but this may quite easily be attributed to the fact that the novel is really a murder mystery, that just happens to be set in the middle of the conflict. In fact, we do not even witness a single war scene until we are well over half way into the story. The action takes place over a much shorter time-frame than most other First World War novels, which tend to encompass a great deal more of the action of the conflict. However, Ben Elton has made up for this, by mentioning, in passing, almost every aspect of the war, which sometimes gives this novel a stifling air within the narrative. Where other authors allow their stories to flow, *The First Casualty* can frequently become bogged down by historical detail, facts and figures. So, although everything here takes place within a few weeks, in the high summer of 1917, we have mentioned, among other subjects: war poets, homosexuals, field punishments, shell-shock, air-raids, complacency on the home front; the causes of the conflict; conditions in the trenches; suffragettes; bombardments; treatment of wounds; losses on the Somme; the mud and rain of Passchendaele; lice; raids on enemy trenches and so on. Because of this sheer weight of information, I have broken this sub-chapter down into different sections, comparing Ben Elton's handling of several subjects, with other authors within this genre.

TRENCH SCENES

When Kingsley first arrives in the trenches, rather than being described in vivid detail, we are told by Ben Elton, in very dry terms how the men are rotated in and out of the lines and the way in which the trenches have been dug: 'a sensible' arrangement of traverses, described in tones of their usefulness. This reads very much like a passage from a secondary school history text book, which spoils the narrative flow of the story and takes up less than a couple of paragraphs, leaving the reader a little confused. It would be interesting to know how Kingsley feels upon seeing the trenches for the first time. The sights, smells and sounds must have some effect on him - surely?

Other authors obviously have to describe trench scenes and Sebastian Barry, in *A Long Long Way,* like many others, is concerned with the feelings of his central characters. So, rather than giving us a description of Willie Dunne's first visit to a trench, he tells us that the event makes Willie feel 'small enough. The biggest thing there was the roaring of Death and the smallest thing was a man.' There is something almost poetic in Barry's language and, although he actually tells us nothing whatsoever about the physical attributes of a trench, he makes the assumption that most people will be sufficiently familiar with images of that war, that they will not need to be told that it is a hole in the ground. They won't need a vivid description of mud and sandbags, duckboards and dugouts, because what really matters to his story is that young Willie Dunne from Dublin is completely terrified.

In Sebastian Faulks's *Birdsong*, the reader has a different introduction to the trenches, as here we do not see the characters arriving fresh from England. Instead, we join them in 1916, as seasoned soldiers, mid-way through a tour of duty. Since none of their surroundings are new to them, the trenches, dugouts and underground tunnels are not described as fresh sights, but in passing, as we go along. However, because these men are, perhaps, more war-weary, we are given much more vivid descriptions of the things they they do notice. For example, when Jack Firebrace expects to be court-martialled for falling asleep on duty, he looks 'up at the rim of the world that was appearing through the grey light: the burned and blasted trees, the once-green fields, now uniformly brown, where all the earth had been turned by shells'. We are told that 'he was reconciled to leaving' this place, because he was so convinced that he would shortly be facing a firing squad. Faulks goes on to describe the dugout in which Firebrace faces the officer, who subsequently excuses his misdemeanour, but this is done with a purpose and brevity which while informative, does not disturb the flow of the story.

In her novel *Strange Meeting*, Susan Hill employs an entirely different method of describing the trenches, in that one of her central characters, David Barton, writes a letter home, in which he gives an account of his first experience of life in the front line. Here we learn about the 'shocking' march to the front, the 'fat and fit looking' rats that are 'scurrying about the whole time', which Barton compares to the mice that he 'used to secrete' about the house as a child. The dugout, we are told, is 'tiny', with 'two bunks of wire netting' and here they all huddle together during bombardments, although Barton feels safer out in the flooded trench. These descriptions are interspersed with accounts of the actions of some of the men, and childhood recollections and other remembrances, so although we do learn a lot about life in the trenches, it doesn't feel forced or contrived. Naturally, because this has been included as part of a letter, the descriptions seem much more human than those which are given in simple narrative terms.

Regeneration by Pat Barker, on the other hand, is mainly set at Craiglockhart Military Hospital in Edinburgh, but we are offered a glimpse of the trenches through another unusual method. This time, the central character, Billy Prior, cannot remember the trauma which caused his breakdown and Dr Rivers reluctantly decides to hypnotise him. While in a trance, Billy recalls the situation in the trenches, which led to his neurosis and in doing so, we are offered a brief description of the surroundings. Here the author has made the assumption that the reader has some degree of imagination, so everything is described in military terms. She tells us about 'funk holes', 'fire bays', 'standing to', 'gas curtains' etc., with absolutely no explanation of any of these terms. However, this makes perfect sense, since these are Billy's recollections and he is an experienced soldier, who would be unlikely to pepper his speech with unnecessary elucidations. Although these latter two pieces might be said to be less informative to the novice reader of First World War literature, there is no doubt that they provide much more realistic descriptions of trenches and trench life, because of the informality of the delivery method.

SEX SCENES

In the matter of sex scenes, I actually find Ben Elton's writing style and language quite surprising. I had expected this to be a no-holds-barred description of exactly who puts what into where, made perhaps slightly comical or crude by his use of coarse language. Instead, we are given various degrees of farcical, romantic melodrama, which lack detail and description to the point where the sex itself seems completely irrelevant and insignificant. This, of course it is not, since it involves Kingsley's seemingly uncharacteristic betrayal of his beloved and beautiful wife. Even if we cannot, for some reason, be given the details of the physical connection, we must be allowed to understand the emotional tie that binds Kingsley to Nurse Murray. Other than the incredibly facile reasons offered: namely her prettiness and his being rather well-endowed, what exactly makes our hero want to keep betraying his wife, despite his avowed regret, and why does Nurse Murray, who despises men in general and policemen in particular, fall head over heels in love with the intrepid inspector?

We are told nothing about how they feel, or why; no reasons are offered as to why these two behave in ways which seem so uncharacteristic. Perhaps it is simply that the sex is so great, that they are carried away and just can't keep their hands off each other. That's perfectly plausible, but how would we know? The detail is missing and without that, this part of the story makes no sense.

As to the language employed in these scenes, it is surprisingly coy, especially given the date of publication. By 2005, even if one limits oneself just to the genre of First World War literature, other authors had already given us great and graphic details of sexual encounters, both heterosexual and homosexual, so there can have been no censorship issues to hinder Ben Elton. However, even if there had been, the employment of such phrases as 'straining manhood', 'Murray's taut young body against his', and the incomparable, '"Golly. That is a big one, isn't it?"' make these amorous scenes laughable. Elton's language is disproportionately chaste, with overtones of giggling schoolboy embarrassment, whereas these episodes should have been given greater significance either by the author's use of more appropriate, or colloquial language, or - perhaps better still - by his metaphorically 'closing the bedroom door' and leaving the sex itself to the reader's imagination. In this way, he could have, perhaps revealed its significance later on, through the characters' recollections or reactions.

As mentioned earlier, other authors, equally unrestricted by censorship difficulties, have also decided to include sex scenes in their First World War novels. In Sebastian Faulks's *Birdsong*, a great deal of the first part of the novel is taken up with the sexual liaison between Stephen Wraysford and Isabelle Azaire four years before the war. As the wife of his French host, Isabelle is very much out-of-bounds, as far as Stephen is concerned, yet this, coupled with her beauty and the sultry atmosphere of a long, hot summer, has the opposite effect, serving only to arouse him further. His feelings for her are a 'force' which cannot 'be stopped'; his desire is a 'necessity' which cannot be denied, to the point where he contemplates achieving his aims even without her consent - in other words, we are led to believe, Stephen is considering rape.

Ultimately, there is no need for such drastic action, as Isabelle willingly consents and they embark upon their illicit affair. Faulks offers vivid and detailed descriptions of their relationship in both physical and emotional terms, mainly because he is trying to convey the enormous significance of their love upon his central character, Stephen Wraysford. This is a passionate, consuming and ultimately destructive affair but, nonetheless, the language employed by the author is still somewhat reserved. Their are no colloquialisms used here, but equally nothing is given its proper name either, which leads to an odd combination of constrained detail. We can easily understand everything that this couple do to each other, but because of the use of language such as 'his gross excitement' and 'the part of him she wanted', which is Faulks's distracting way of describing Wraysford's penis, their affair takes on the air of romantic fiction, which is a little inappropriate. Eventually, this consuming relationship devours them both: Isabelle leaves Stephen and returns to her husband and at this point the reader should have a true, deep understanding of Stephen's utter devastation, as he grows 'cold' with despair. However, the sex scenes - which are their only real connection - have become repetitive and mechanical, as though the author had run out of lyrical descriptions for the human anatomy and, because of this, these portrayals lack the passion which we are supposed to believe Stephen feels he has lost.

Pat Barker's *Regeneration Trilogy* features many sex scenes, written so explicitly that some might even call them offensive. The central character throughout the trilogy, Billy Prior, is a confused, troubled young man and this is reflected in his sexual relationships and behaviour which, by his own admission can sometimes be mixed up with his nightmares about the war. In *Regeneration*, Billy is learning to control himself following his breakdown, and his sexual liaisons are very much along those lines: he wants to be in charge and everything must be on his terms. His relationship with Sarah Lumb, however becomes quite significant and by the end of the novel, he is 'in love'. Throughout the trilogy, sex between Billy and Sarah is always treated differently to sex between Billy and anyone else.

As soon as *The Eye in the Door* opens, we learn that, while sex is of great significance to Billy, fidelity is not, as he tries to persuade a young women named Myra into greater intimacy than she wishes. When this fails, Billy tries his luck, with much greater success, on a fellow officer, Charles Manning. Their homosexual encounter is very graphically portrayed, leaving nothing to the imagination and making the reader very aware of Billy's sadistic nature. Later, when Billy and Sarah meet again, their sex scene is described in more loving and romantic tones, clearly - in fact, rather too obviously - demonstrating that this is the more significant emotional relationship.

In *The Ghost Road*, Pat Barker takes this contrast to another level, as sex between Billy and Sarah is described in the present tense, demonstrating that, while they are together, nothing else matters to Billy, except the here and now. Sex with other people, whether male or female, is still coarse and perfunctory, the descriptions here showing that these liaisons are simply a means to sexual gratification and have no emotional claim on Billy.

Somewhere in between the somehow inappropriate romanticism of Faulks or Elton and the raw crudeness of Pat Barker, there lies Sebastian Barry, who in his novel *A Long Long Way*, employs another method of describing sex. Here, we are shown a relationship between Willie Dunne and Gretta Lawlor, which is evidently of great emotional importance to Willie. He proposes marriage twice and the reader is left with no doubt that Gretta is the love of his life. The physical side of their relationship, however, is left entirely to the reader's imagination. We know that sexual relations take place, but we are told absolutely nothing: it is as though that side of their relationship is private and none of our business. This actually has the effect of making this liaison seem more significant and realistic, since later in the novel, Barry doesn't hold back in describing in crude and graphic detail, the events which take place when Willie and one of his comrades visit a brothel. So, we know that the author's reticence in providing details about Willie and Gretta's relationship has nothing to do with prudishness on his part - which means he is trying to tell us something else by his omission. This might work better if we understood more about the characters. However, in this case, the author has provided us with almost no information regarding Willie or Gretta, so it actually falls flat as a literary device. This is a shame, as otherwise, this might have proved successful.

Censorship obviously makes a great difference as to how an author may deal with sexual encounters and, in this respect, the earlier First World War novels differ greatly from those written in the last quarter of the twentieth century, and subsequently. In *All Quiet on the Western Front*, which was published in 1929, Erich Maria Remarque hints at sexual acts taking place, but the detail is omitted. On one occasion, the central character, Paul Baumer and two of his comrades take food to three French women, in return for which they are offered sex. Paul builds this event up to something really meaningful and significant, not wanting to compare this action with the time spent in military-approved brothels, the thought of which he immediately regrets and tries to banish. In this way, Remarque lets us know that sex is on the agenda. He also mentions Paul's feelings of awe 'at the sight of my clear skin when the light of the lamp falls upon it', telling us that nakedness has entered the scene. This really is the limit of the physical description, other than a couple of kisses. Instead, Remarque describes Paul's thoughts and fears. He looks upon this act as an opportunity to forget 'war terror and grossness' and longs to 'awaken young and happy', which is quite an important statement from a character who is only nineteen years old. However, afterwards, reality dawns and he is forced to admit: 'I am not in the least happy' and although he and his friends laugh as they return to their billets, one senses that Paul regrets this liaison, probably because he had been seeking an emotional liaison which he failed to find, but also because at the end of it, the war was still there and nothing had changed.

DEATH

Perhaps one of the most significant aspects of any First World War novel is the way in which the author deals with death. This is a pivotal part of any war story, whether it be from the perspective of killing, loss or the actual experience of seeing deaths in battle. In Kingsley, we have an unusual character when it comes to this topic, since as a conscientious objector, he might have hoped to escape the ordeal of witnessing death at first hand. It is not that Kingsley is squeamish, as he has sent criminals to the gallows, but we don't really know how he will react to being in the immediate vicinity of such 'unimaginable daily slaughter', or perhaps even being directly responsible for it.

Sometimes we don't actually need to be given very much detail about an actual death scene to understand its significance: what we really require is a description of the reactions of the characters involved. So, when Kingsley is going up through the trenches to find Captain Edmonds and a bomb goes off just behind him, killing or wounding almost everyone in sight, what we really need is to understand how this brutal introduction to war makes Kingsley feel. Instead, Ben Elton offers a diatribe on the 'arbitrary' nature of the war, after which Kingsley simply leaves the area.

A very similar scene is described in Pat Barker's *Regeneration*, where Billy Prior recounts to Dr Rivers, while under the influence of hypnosis, the events which led to his breakdown. Again, he had been walking through the trenches and a bomb had exploded shortly after he had passed through. Pat Barker does not offer very much more detail as to the physical effects of the bomb blast than Ben Elton, but what she does give us are Billy's reactions, as he clears up the debris. Despite the fact that this is Billy's recollection, it is still written in the third person, which ought to make it less personal, although the reader still feels drawn into Billy's dreadful experience, which leads eventually, to him sitting 'on the bench, his clasped hands dangling between his legs', thinking of nothing. Worse is to follow, however, when Billy wakes from his trance, back into the real world. He is incredulous, wondering how such a 'trivial' experience could have broken him and he begins to cry uncontrollably, beating his head against the chest of Dr Rivers. This secondary breakdown is, if anything, more shocking, as we know how out of character this emotional reaction is, but also because we know that Billy's trench experience was anything but 'trivial'. By seeing this trauma through someone else's eyes and seeing the reaction as we do, it becomes extremely personal, even though it is written in the way it is, and despite the fact that there is actually very little description of the event itself.

Another such scene is described in *Birdsong* by Sebastian Faulks. Here, a shell lands in the trench, burying several men, who are dug out by the central character, Stephen Wraysford, among others. Some of these men are terribly wounded and their injuries are graphically described by the author. At one stage, Wraysford tries to staunch the flow of blood gushing from the wounds of a man named Douglas and in doing so, feels his hand slipping in through the wound 'towards the man's lung'. Wraysford becomes saturated with blood, which has a smell like 'the back of a butcher's shop, only stronger', as it flows up his arms, into his hair and soaks through his trousers. Eventually, Wraysford becomes hysterical, screaming at the stretcher bearers to remove Douglas and '"Get this man's blood off me"'. Throughout this passage, the reader is in no doubt that Wraysford will be deeply affected by this experience.

By the very nature of the First World War, death was often accompanied by decay and this is another aspect of the conflict upon which novelists often touch. Here, descriptions are essential to the reader's understanding, since it is very difficult for us to imagine the sights and smells that accompany decomposing corpses. In *The First Casualty*, Ben Elton mentions this topic in Chapter forty-two, when Kingsley follows Captain Edmonds and his men on the raid. Realising that he has not 'blacked-up' his face, Kingsley reaches down into the mud to 'gather up some earth' and finds instead that he has 'stuck his hand through the body of a maggot-ridden corpse'. He then wipes his hand on his 'already gory greatcoat' and continues on his way. This tells us nothing about the sensation of plunging one's hands into a rotting body. Where is the sense of smell? Was there no escape of gas from the body? How did the flesh feel to the touch? A little later, Kingsley removes a bullet from a newly killed body, which would have given the author the perfect opportunity to compare the two experiences, instead of which, all we are told is that a 'fresh' body is 'not so easy to penetrate'.

In *Birdsong*, Sebastian Faulks offers a very different perspective of the decaying corpse. Wraysford and some of his men, including one named Brennan go out into No Man's Land to 'bring back some bodies'. This is an odious task, which the men despise, although Wraysford is less perturbed, pointing out that 'It's only death'. As they begin their task, the situation becomes almost humourous, as some men are told to take the arms of one corpse, only to find that the limbs literally come away in their hands. Flies, which have covered the bodies, rise up, disturbed, 'transforming black skin... into green by their absence.' The men use empty sandbags over their hands to protect them from the slimy, spongy, rotting flesh, as they gather identity discs. Rats peek out between the corpses 'glutted with pleasure'. Then Brennan grabs hold of one particular body: headless and legless, and drags it 'up from the crater, his fingers vanishing into buttered green flesh'. The author then simply reveals: 'It was his brother.' This shocking scene and its final revelation are made more realistic by Faulks's use of simple, every-day language, so the reader can imagine this episode with relative ease. The story of the scene is then completed by the author telling us of the mens' reactions to this experience. One man alternates between vomiting and weeping; another sits with a 'rigid smile'; Brennan, meanwhile, tells a concerned Wraysford that he feels 'better'; he feels 'lucky', because he brought his brother back and 'now he'll have a proper burial'. There is a calmness and serenity about these words and this aftermath, which make it necessarily and justifiably haunting.

As a conscientious objector, we may safely assume that Kingsley had never intended to take a life when he agreed to undertake the commission offered to him by Sir Mansfield Cumming. To do so would be contrary to his beliefs, and yet within moments of entering the enemy's trench during the raid, that is precisely what Kingsley does. This is hardly surprising, since he is placed in the position of having to kill the enemy, or be killed himself. Nonetheless, this is an extremely significant moment for Kingsley and afterwards, he argues with himself that he has been a hypocrite; that he has sacrificed family, freedom and career 'on a point of principle', which he has now 'tossed aside'. He now has the 'blood of at least ten Germans' on his hands and this, evidently, haunts him. Or that is what we are supposed to believe. However, the idea that Kingsley is in any way damaged or even altered by this experience is impossible to conceive, since we know nothing of the deaths he has caused, or of his feelings about them. As he shoots each man, the only thing we know, is the position in which Kingsley stands; that each man is (miraculously) shot 'between the eyes', and that Kingsley always 'thinks' before acting. This tells us absolutely nothing and yet we are supposed to believe that these deaths prey on his conscience. Where is the blood? Where is the description of each man's expression as he falls? Why does each one have to die in exactly the same way? Wouldn't it be more realistic if at least one of them could be shot somewhere else? With so much missing and such a lack of realism and humanity, I find it very hard to believe that Kingsley was even remotely bothered about these deaths.

Very much the same thing happens in Sebastian Barry's *A Long Long Way*, where Willie Dunne is responsible for the death of a German soldier during a gas attack. He later buries this German and, we are told by the author, he is haunted by this memory - even at the point of his own death. This makes no sense at all really, as the event of the German soldier's death is so scantily described, as is his burial, during which the supposedly 'haunted' Willie daydreams about Dublin. This is Willie's 'first German' - hence the importance of this experience - and yet, with so little detail, the reader cannot be expected to treat this episode as one of any great significance.

I suppose that one could argue that there is always the possibility that first-hand experience might be the telling factor which adds realism to such scenes, and this would certainly seem to be the case in *All Quiet on the Western Front* by Erich Maria Remarque. Here, Paul Baumer stabs a French soldier with his knife and then has to sit in a shell-hole and watch his victim slowly die. Initially Paul tries to ignore him, then he helps, bandaging the wound he created. Eventually the Frenchman dies and Paul goes through his pockets, discovering small details about the man's life before the war and making idle promises to himself about what he will achieve, to make amends for his 'crime', if he should survive the war. Remarque takes pages and pages describing this event and Paul's reactions, giving it and its consequences due deference, because it changes Paul and we must be allowed to understand why.

However, it is not only those with first hand experience who can achieve this quality of writing and it does not always require pages and pages of words. Sometimes, we can be made to understand the significance of an event by what is not said. However it must be not said in a certain way for this to work. So, where Elton and Barry have gone wrong, Pat Barker has triumphed. *In The Ghost Road*, Billy Prior returns to France (together with Wilfred Owen) and begins to keep a diary. On October 4th, he writes about a battle in which they have participated and over the ensuing couple of days, continues to reveal more of these recent events. However, when it comes to killing, he says almost nothing. He talks of 'bayonet work. Which I will not remember.' He recalls the sight of Owen killing others, but knows they won't talk about this, or his own memories of 'the faces of the men I killed in the counter-attack.' Apart from that, he says nothing about taking life, although he mentions the deaths of his own comrades. This stunning diary shows the reality of war: the camaraderie, loss, self-deceit, triumph of survival and above all - and perhaps most strangely but realistically of all, the beauty - not of war, but of life.

FURTHER READING
RECOMMENDATIONS FOR STUDENTS

Students are often expected to demonstrate a sound knowledge of the texts which they are studying and also to enhance this knowledge with extensive reading of other books within this genre. I have provided on the following pages a list of books, poetry, plays and non-fiction which, in my opinion, provide a good basic understanding of this topic. In addition, a small review of each book has been provided to help students choose which of the following are most suitable for them.

NOVELS

BIRDSONG by Sebastian Faulks

Written in 1993, this novel tells the story of Stephen Wraysford, his destructive pre-war love-affair, his war experiences and, through the eyes of his grand-daughter, the effects of the war on his personality and his generation. A central theme to this story is man's ability to overcome adversity: to rise above his circumstances and survive - no matter what is thrown in his path. Many readers find the first part of this novel difficult to get through, but it is worth persevering. The pre-war section of the novel is essential in the understanding of Stephen Wraysford's character and his reactions to the events which happen later. Faulks's descriptions of battle scenes are among the best in this genre. In our view, this novel is suitable only for A-Level students, due to some adult themes.

A VERY LONG ENGAGEMENT by Sebastien Japrisot

A story of enduring love, truth and determination. Refusing to believe that her fiancé can possibly have left her forever, Mathilde decides to search for Manech whom she has been told is missing, presumed dead. She learns from a first-hand witness, that he may not have died, so she sets out on a voyage of discovery - learning not just about his fate, but also a great deal about herself and human nature. Mathilde herself has to overcome her own personal fears and hardships and, out of sheer persistence and a refusal to accept the obvious, she eventually discovers the truth. Although this novel does not form part of the main syllabus reading list, it does make an interesting and fairly easy read and is useful from the perspective that it gives a French woman's viewpoint of the war.

REGENERATION by Pat Barker

This book is, as its title implies, a novel about the rebuilding of men following extreme trauma. Billy Prior is a young working-class officer - a 'temporary gentleman' - who finds himself at Craiglockhart Military Hospital in Edinburgh, having been damaged by his experiences on the Western Front. It is the job of Dr W. H. R. Rivers, to 'mend' Prior, and others like him, ready for them to return to the fighting, while wrestling with his own conscience at the same time. Interweaved into this central plot is the meeting, also at Craiglockhart, of poets Siegfried Sassoon and Wilfred Owen, who are both there to receive treatment. This mixture of fact and fiction within a novel has created some controversy, but it is a common feature within this genre and one which Pat Barker handles better than most. This is an immensely useful book - even if not read as part of the Trilogy - as it takes place away from the front lines, showing the reader the deep and long-lasting effects of battle upon men, whose lives would never be the same again. Due to some adult content, we recommend this book for A-Level students only.

THE RETURN OF THE SOLDIER by Rebecca West

Written in 1918, by an author who had lived through the conflict, this home-front novel gives a useful insight into the trauma of war and society's reaction, as seen through the eyes of three women. Chris Baldry, an officer and husband of Kitty, returns home mid-way through the war, suffering from shell-shock and amnesia. He believes that that he is still in a relationship with Margaret Allington - his first love from fifteen years earlier. Kitty, Margaret and Chris's cousin, Jenny, must decide whether to leave Chris in his make-believe world, safe from the war; or whether to 'cure' him and risk his future welfare once he returns to being a soldier. A useful novel from many perspectives in that it was written right at the end of the war, and it gives a female, home-front view of the effects of the war on individuals and families.

ALL QUIET ON THE WESTERN FRONT by Erich Maria Remarque

Written from first-hand experience of life in the trenches, this novel is the moving account of the lives of a group of young German soldiers during the First World War. Remarque had been in the trenches during the later stages of the war and this poignant account of war is a must-read for all those who show an interest in this subject. His descriptions of trench-life and battles are second-to-none and his portrayal of the close friendships forged between the men make this an immensely valuable piece of literature. The fact that this, often shocking, story is told from a German perspective also demonstrates the universal horrors of the war and the sympathy between men of both sides for others enduring the same hardships as themselves.

A LONG LONG WAY by Sebastian Barry

Sebastian Barry's novel tells the a story of Willie Dunne, a young Irish volunteer serving in the trenches of the Western Front. Willie must not only contend with the horrors of the war, but also his own confused feelings regarding the Easter uprising of 1916, and his father's disapproval. Willie's feelings and doubts lead to great upheavals in his life, including personal losses and betrayals by those whom he had believed he could trust. This is an interesting novel about loyalty, war and love, although it does suffer from a degree of historical inaccuracy. In our opinion, due to the adult content of this novel, it is suitable only for A-Level students.

NOT SO QUIET... by Helen Zenna Smith

This novel describes the lives of women working very close to the front line on the Western Front during the First World War, as ambulance drivers. Theirs is a dangerous job, in harsh conditions, with little or no respite. Helen (or Smithy, as she is called by her friends), eventually breaks down under the pressure of the work and returns, briefly, to England. An excellent novel for studying the female perspective, as well as the home front.

POETRY

It is recommended that students read from a wide variety of poets, including female writers. The following anthologies provide good resources for students.

POEMS OF THE FIRST WORLD WAR -
NEVER SUCH INNOCENCE
Edited by Martin Stephen

Probably one of the finest anthologies of First World War poetry currently available. Martin Stephen has collected together some of the best known works by some of the most famous and well-read poets and mixed these with more obscure verses, including many by women and those on the home-front, together with some popular songs both from home and from the front. These have been interspersed with excellent notes which give the reader sufficient information without being too weighty. At the back of the book, there are short biographical notes on many of the poets. This is a fine anthology, suitable both for those who are starting out with their studies, and for the more experienced reader.

LADS: LOVE POETRY OF THE TRENCHES by Martin Taylor

Featuring many lesser-known poets and poems, this anthology approaches the First World War from a different perspective: love. A valuable introduction discusses the emotions of men who, perhaps for the first time, were discovering their own capacity to love their fellow man. This is not an anthology of purely homo-erotic poems, but also features verses by those who had found affection and deep, lasting friendship in the trenches of the First World War.

SCARS UPON MY HEART
Selected by Catherine Reilly

First published in 1981, this anthology is invaluable as it features a collection of poems written exclusively by women on the subject of the First World War. Some of the better known female poets are featured here, such as Vera Brittain and Jessie Pope, but there are also many more writers who are less famous. In addition there are some poets whose work is featured, who are not now renowned for their poetry, but for their works in other areas of literature. Many of the poets included here have minor biographical details featured at the end of the anthology. This book has become the 'standard' for those wishing to study the female contribution to this genre.

UP THE LINE TO DEATH
Edited by Brian Gardner

This anthology, described by its editor Brian Gardner as a 'book about war', is probably, and deservedly, one of the most widely read in this genre. The famous and not-so-famous sit happily together within in these pages of carefully selected poetry. Arranged thematically, these poems provide a poet's-eye-view of the progression of the war, from the initial euphoria and nationalistic pride of John Freeman's 'Happy is England Now' to Sassoon's plea that we should 'never forget'. Useful biographical details and introductions complete this book, which is almost certainly the most useful and important of all the First World War poetry anthologies.

NON-FICTION

UNDERTONES OF WAR by Edmund Blunden

Edmund Blunden's memoir of his experiences in the First World War is a moving, enlightening and occasionally humorous book, demonstrating above all the intense feelings of respect and comradeship which Blunden found in the trenches.

MEMOIRS OF AN INFANTRY OFFICER by Siegfried Sassoon

Following on from *Memoirs of a Fox-hunting Man*, this book is an
autobiographical account of Sassoon's life during the First World War. Sassoon
has changed the names of the characters and George Sherston (Sassoon) is not a
poet. Sassoon became one of the war's most famous poets and this prose
account of his war provides useful background information.
(For a list of the fictional characters and their factual counterparts, see Appendix
II of *Siegfried Sassoon* by John Stuart Roberts.)

THE GREAT WAR GENERALS ON THE WESTERN FRONT 1914-1918 by Robin Neillands

Like many others before and since, the cover of this book claims that it will
dismiss the old myth that the troops who served in the First World War were
badly served by their senior officers. Unlike most of the other books, however,
this one is balanced and thought-provoking. Of particular interest within this
book is the final chapter which provides an assessment of the main protagonists
and their role in the conflict.

THE WESTERN FRONT by Richard Holmes

This is one of many history books about the First World War. Dealing specifically
with the Western Front, Richard Holmes looks at the creation of the trench
warfare system, supplying men and munitions, major battles and living on the
front line.

LETTERS FROM A LOST GENERATION (FIRST WORLD WAR LETTERS OF VERA BRITTAIN AND FOUR FRIENDS) Edited by Alan Bishop and Mark Bostridge

A remarkable insight into the changes which the First World War caused to a
particular set of individuals. In this instance, Vera Brittain lost four important
people in her life (two close friends, her fiancé and her brother). The agony this
evoked is demonstrated through letters sent between these five characters, which
went on to form the basis of Vera Brittain's autobiography *Testament of Youth*.

1914-1918: VOICES AND IMAGES OF THE GREAT WAR
by Lyn MacDonald

One of the most useful 'unofficial' history books available to those studying the First World War. This book tells the story of the soldiers who fought the war through their letters, diary extracts, newspaper reports, poetry and eye-witness accounts. As with all of Lyn MacDonald's excellent books, *Voices and Images of the Great War* tells its story through the words of the people who were there. The author gives just the right amount of background information of a political and historical nature to keep the reader interested and informed, while leaving the centre-stage to those who really matter... the men themselves.

BIBLIOGRAPHY

STRANGE MEETING by Susan Hill

BIRDSONG by Sebastian Faulks

ALL QUIET ON THE WESTERN FRONT by Erich Maria Remarque

THE RETURN OF THE SOLDIER by Rebecca West

JOURNEY'S END by R C Sherriff

REGENERATION by Pat Barker

THE EYE IN THE DOOR by Pat Barker

THE GHOST ROAD by Pat Barker

A LONG LONG WAY by Sebastian Barry

THE FIRST WORLD WAR by John Keegan

CHRONOLOGY OF THE GREAT WAR, 1914-1918 Edited by Lord Edward Gleichen

THE BRITISH EXPEDITIONARY FORCE 1914-15 by Bruce Gudmundsson

OTHER GREAT WAR LITERATURE STUDY GUIDE TITLES

GREAT WAR LITERATURE STUDY GUIDE E-BOOKS:

NOVELS & PLAYS

All Quiet on the Western Front
Birdsong
Journey's End (A-Level or GCSE)
Regeneration
The Eye in the Door
The Ghost Road
A Long Long Way
The First Casualty
Strange Meeting
The Return of the Soldier
The Accrington Pals
Not About Heroes
Oh What a Lovely War

POET BIOGRAPHIES AND POETRY ANALYSIS:

Herbert Asquith
Harold Begbie
John Peale Bishop
Edmund Blunden
Vera Brittain
Rupert Brooke
Thomas Burke

May Wedderburn Cannan
Margaret Postgate Cole
Alice Corbin
E E Cummings
Nancy Cunard
T S Eliot
Eleanor Farjeon
Gilbert Frankau
Robert Frost
Wilfrid Wilson Gibson
Anna Gordon Keown
Robert Graves
Julian Grenfell
Ivor Gurney
Thomas Hardy
Alan P Herbert
Agnes Grozier Herbertson
W N Hodgson
A E Housman
Geoffrey Anketell Studdert Kennedy
Winifred M Letts
Amy Lowell
E A Mackintosh
John McCrae
Charlotte Mew
Edna St Vincent Millay
Ruth Comfort Mitchell
Harriet Monroe
Edith Nesbit
Robert Nichols
Wilfred Owen
Jessie Pope
Ezra Pound
Florence Ripley Mastin
Isaac Rosenberg
Carl Sandburg
Siegfried Sassoon
Alan Seeger
Charles Hamilton Sorley
Wallace Stevens

Sara Teasdale
Edward Wyndham Tennant
Lesbia Thanet
Edward Thomas
Iris Tree
Katharine Tynan Hinkson
Robert Ernest Vernède
Arthur Graeme West

*Please note that e-books are only available direct from our Web site at
www.greatwarliterature.co.uk and cannot be purchased through bookshops.*

NOTES

NOTES

NOTES

Printed in Great Britain
by Amazon